IN TRANSIT

Mobility, City Culture and Urban Development in Rotterdam

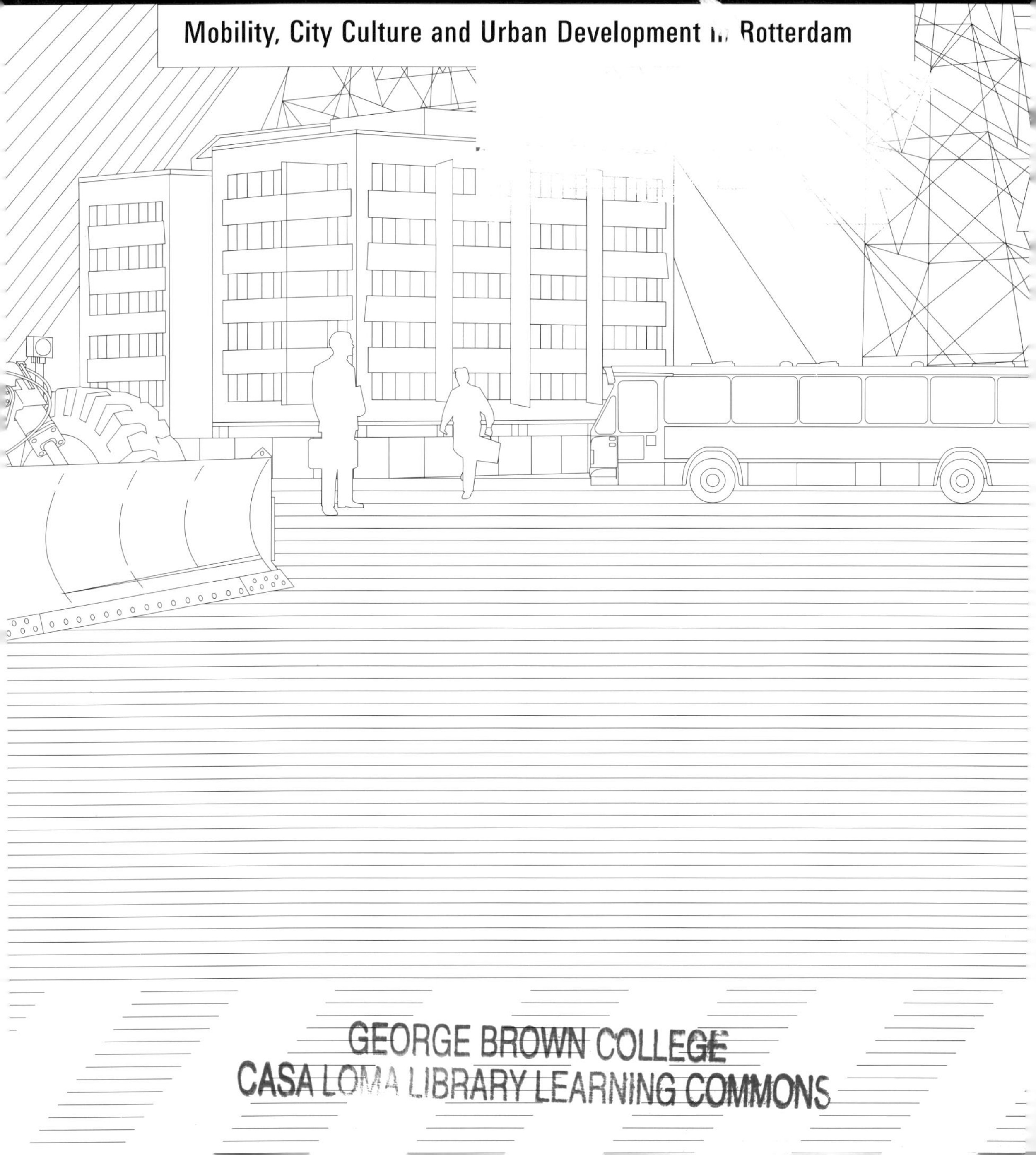

HF
MW01709298
2007 05 14
GEORGE BROWN COLLEGE
CASA LOMA LIBRARY LEARNING COMMONS

Vroooooaam

IN TRANSIT

Mobility, City Culture and Urban Development in Rotterdam

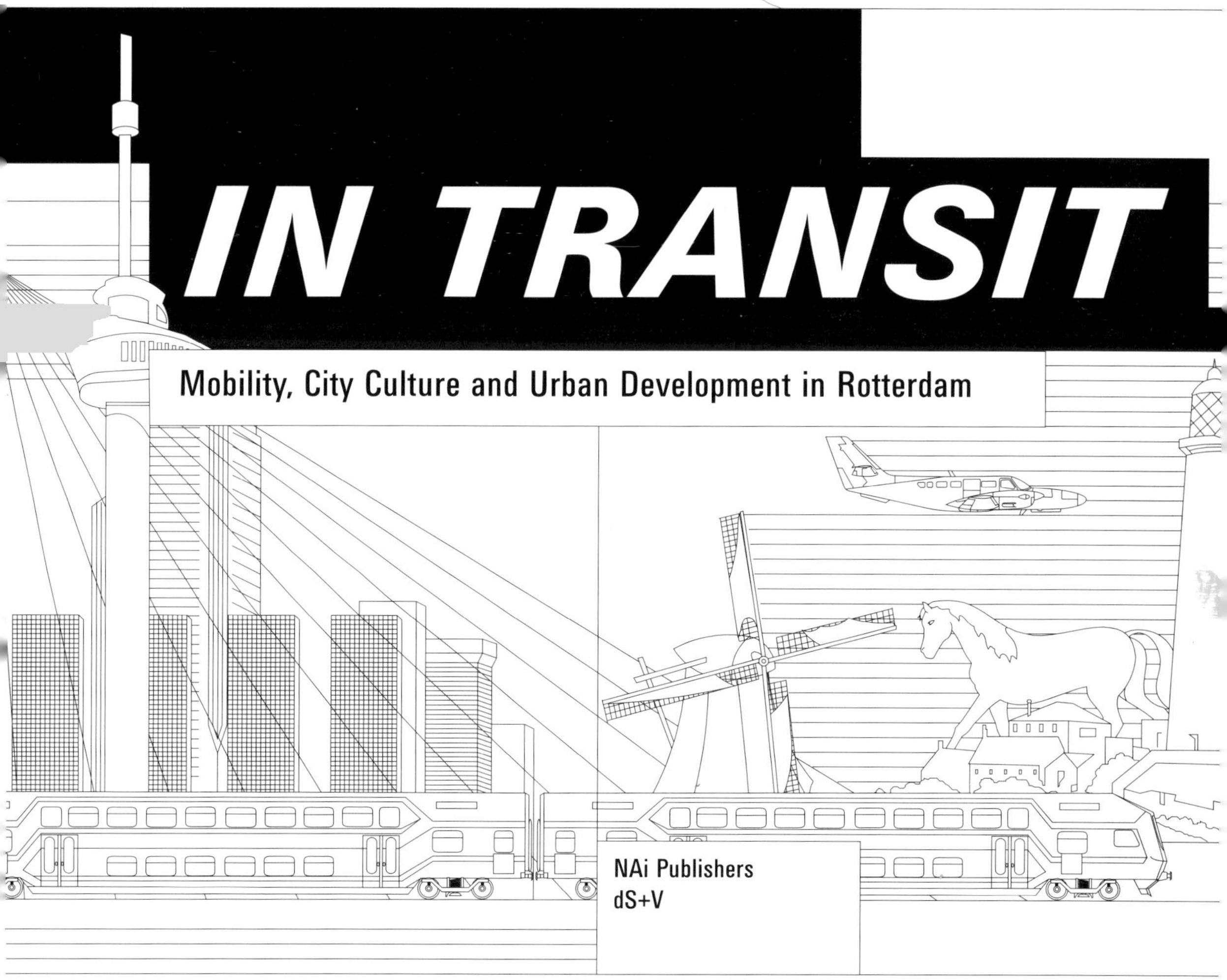

NAi Publishers
dS+V

Editors Paul Meurs and Marc Verheijen

With contributions by Luuk Boelens, Frans Botma, Florian Boer, Dolf Broekhuizen, Martin Guit, Jannes Linders, Paul Meurs, Henk Oosterling, Arnold Reijndorp, Pieter Schrijnen, Harko Stolte, Minke Themans, Bas van Toledo and Marc Verheijen

GEORGE BROWN COLLEGE
CASA LOMA LIBRARY LEARNING COMMONS

CONTENT

Rotterdam as laboratory – the automobile city *par excellence*

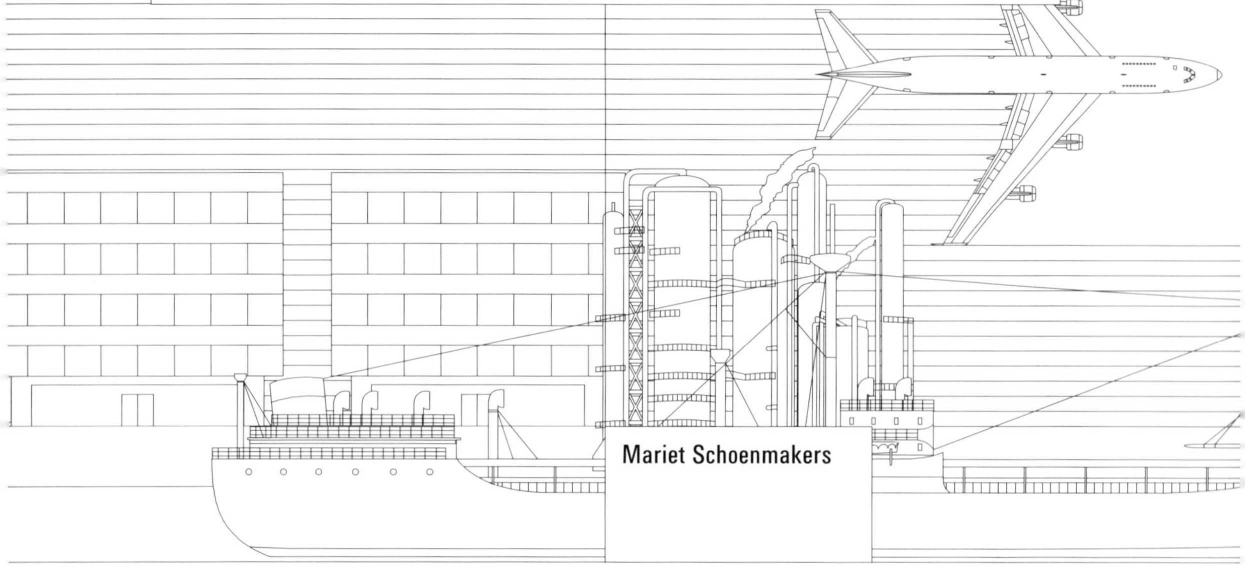

Mariet Schoenmakers

FOREWORD

It seems that humans have an almost physical need to move. We move and we head for a destination. This is what we now call 'mobility'.
What does that movement mean in this epoch, in this city? What are all these forms of mobility heading into the great unknown? What is the spatial experience in a city like Rotterdam, with such a specific sense of space that it seems to have been tailor-made for a moving viewpoint? What is our perception of distance in that space?

In the most widely dispersed city in the Netherlands, movement is the best way to get acquainted with Rotterdam, to see it and feel it. Whether taking in the view from the Brienenoord Bridge, enjoying a boat trip through the Europoort docklands or rolling through the urbanized landscape in a metro carriage – it is a cosmopolitan pleasure. City life is movement; it is encounters with different cultures; it is trade and the port. The people of Rotterdam are urban travellers.

Standing still is of even greater importance in the midst of all that movement. The city at eye-level: waiting for the tram, stopping for a raised bridge. The atmosphere of a place is a feeling that goes beyond words. What do the symbols of mobility add to our urban experience, how do we relate to these icons, and what informs their public function for the urban community? Those are the issues that lie before us, especially as the private life of mobile people is increasingly shaped by the public space. What quality – what beauty – do these new collective spaces have?

This book presents a kaleidoscopic impression of what urbanity is under today's conditions. I hope that it succeeds in bringing together some of the ideas and imagining that Rotterdam inspires, and that it will inspire everyone involved with the design of cities to work together towards new futures and wonderful new spaces.

USER SPACE ROTTERDAM

Jannes Linders

haven
asmus MC
seumpark

STOP BUSH

MAERSK

Esso
McDRIVE
DELFT-NOORD
DE WAARHEID

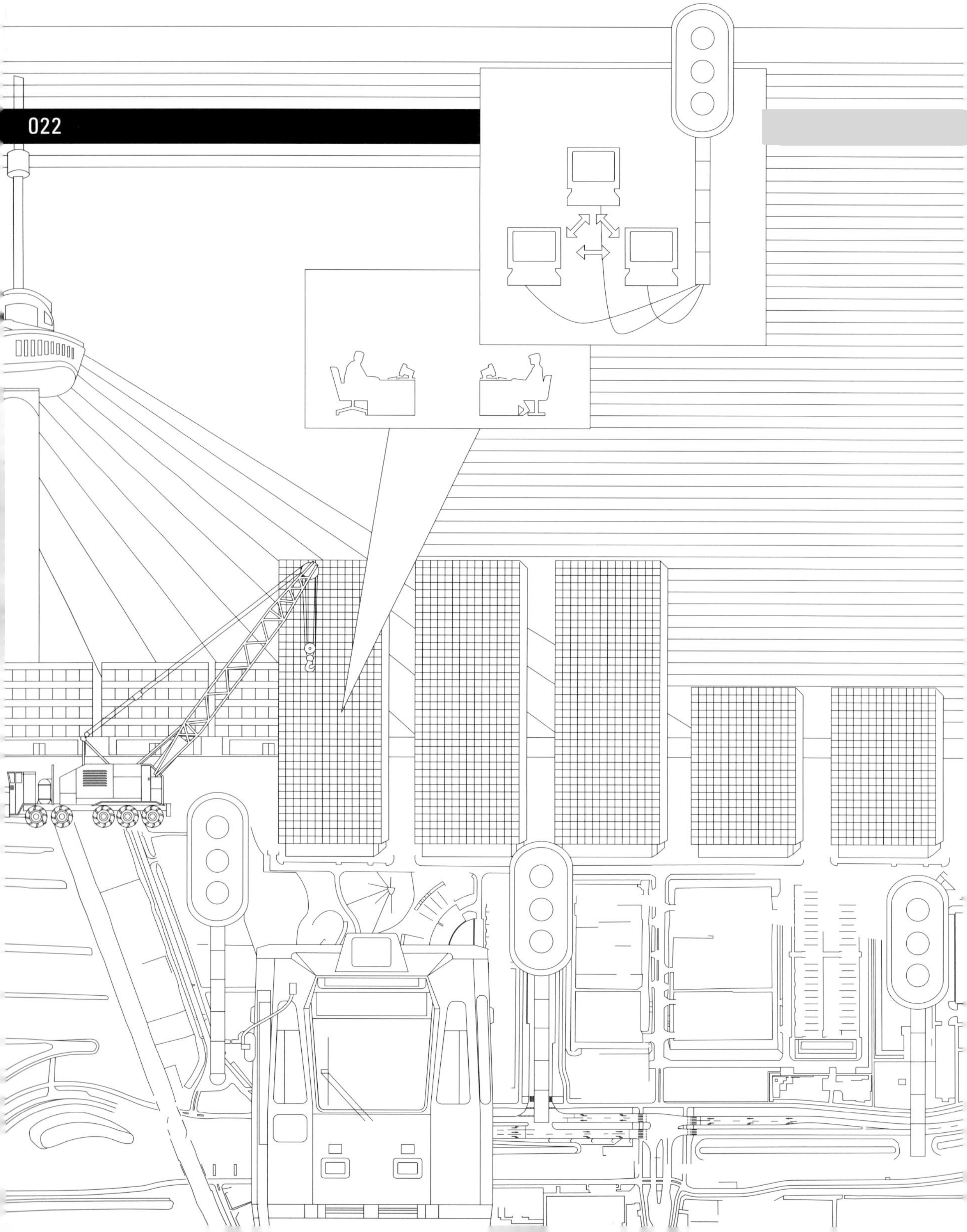

INTRODUCTION

Paul Meurs

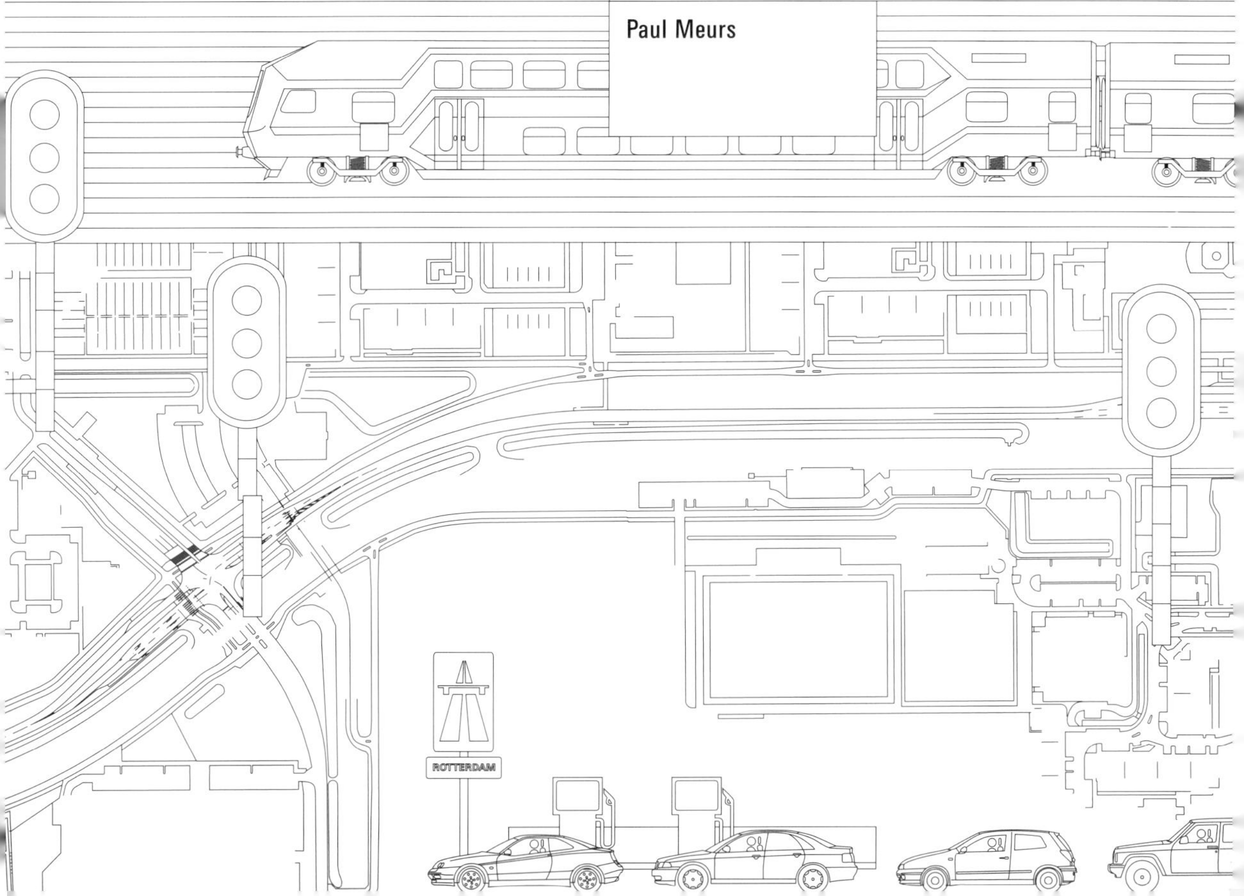

In one of the tower blocks on Rotterdam's Marconiplein, there is a room packed with computers and monitors. It is from here that the traffic flows in the city are monitored: the nerve centre of the Dynamic Traffic Management system. Every hour, the central computer 'phones' each of the city's 237 sets of traffic lights to make sure that all is well. If not, or when a traffic signal reports a problem to the control room between the regular checks, a call is automatically made to one of the four departments responsible for maintenance. And so the traffic system is kept operational around the clock, seven days a week. The constant stream of data from the city to Marconiplein forms the input for all manner of graphs, bar charts and flow diagrams, which then allow constant adjustment of the system to optimize the progress of traffic on the roads of Rotterdam. On the traffic managers' monitors, Rotterdam's traffic system certainly seems very hi-tech. The unsuspecting visitor finds himself in a veritable 'Mission Control'. However, the actual situation on the streets is rather more down to earth. The traffic lights do their best to pump the traffic through the city as efficiently as possible, but the lines of cars, cyclists and trams still tend to move in fits and starts. Occasionally there are serious accidents, resulting in delays and frayed tempers. In the rush hour (which is never actually one hour but a substantial portion of every morning, evening and weekend)
the infrastructure cogs can turn very slowly indeed. The effects are many: clouds of pollution, unacceptable levels of noise. People become hot and bothered, a nd the city grinds to a halt. Gridlock. This problem is not unique to Rotterdam. The situation is little better anywhere else. Traffic on the motorways slows to walking pace almost every day, public transport fails to arrive on time (or at all), the airports are full to overflowing and bus services to outlying areas have been cut back or discontinued. Accessibility is a 'hot item' which enjoys a prominent position on the political agenda.

From traffic to mobility

Good accessibility is essential to the economy and is generally regarded as a basic requirement of society. In the twentieth century, strictly ordered spatial planning was meant to provide the key to the optimum functioning of towns and cities. Separation of functions was the watchword, with planners drawing distinct divisions between the familiar quartet of homes, business, recreation and transport. Until the early 1990s, the word 'mobility' was rarely heard. Until then, people referred to 'the traffic problem'. Attention turned to the more fluid processing of traffic flows, an undertaking which became the domain of the 'Traffic Management Consultant'.
Today, it is all too clear that traffic managers and engineers have failed to do enough to ensure efficient flows of people and goods around the country. Each year, millions of euros are invested in railways, special peak-hour congestion lanes, road widening schemes, by passes, new roads and advanced traffic regulation technologies. Nevertheless, accessibility has declined rather than improved, particularly within and between the economic centres. Neither has the traditional strategy of discouraging car use and promoting public transport had the desired effect. True enough, the trains are full to overflowing, but the growth in car ownership and 'automobility' has continued unchecked for the better part of a century. Each new road, each widened lane generates yet more traffic,

whereupon resolving one bottleneck merely serves to create another elsewhere. In this situation, smothering the country in yet more asphalt will have little effect. Only when traffic is viewed in a wider context than that of traffic management alone, taking economic, social and spatial developments into consideration, will there be any hope of gaining control over the traffic flows in and around the cities. This is where the concept of 'mobility' comes in. Mobility is not so much a science as a social phenomenon. Mobility is so important and so all-embracing that it is difficult to determine exactly where it begins and where it ends. It can apply to practically all aspects of movement from one place to another, whether by a commuter or a refugee. It encompasses issues from social alienation to nomadic lifestyles, from open borders to chatting on the Internet. It touches upon issues of segregation. But above all, mobility remains a question of movement from one place to another, whether to work in another city, a day trip to some remote corner of the country, a long weekend in Paris or a holiday on another continent. Such movement is now more frequent and more rapid. It involves a greater number of people, traversing ever greater distances. And not only people: goods and ideas move from one place to another as well. The effect is known as globalization, whereby good and evil can encircle the world, and can establish themselves anywhere and everywhere. Increasing mobility precipitates structural changes to society, and in turn these changes bring about yet further mobility. The impact of mobility is total. Its effects are not only to be seen on the global scale, but at that of countries and regions, and that of the day-to-day lives of individuals. Everyone is affected by mobility, and almost everyone is mobile in one way or another. Mobility is an inseparable part of life's drudgery and its pleasures.

Leaving aside virtual mobility, such as that offered by television and the Internet, physical mobility determines our general perceptions of society. Many people experience a city from a moving perspective, as they themselves move from one place to another. Their impression of the city is determined by what they see and experience along the way. The infrastructure is among the most frequently used of public areas. Here, people meet other people whether they like it or not. Unsafe cycle paths, dilapidated bus shelters or loutish behaviour on the roads are all indicators of social decline and the demise of collective values. Some people no longer feel safe on the streets, and their fears can often be traced back to the feeling that 'something is going to happen' while moving from one place to another. There is a dynamic interaction between mobility and spatial design. Traffic flows have a great influence on the form and subsequent transformations of both urban and rural areas, while conversely, spatial interventions may be necessary in order to influence and control the movement of traffic flows. The traditional 'static city' concept, in which each function is assigned its own area, has given way to the 'dynamic city', in which mobility can no longer be compared to a circulatory system of veins and arteries but forms the very skeleton of the urban organism. It is *movement* that generates and conditions the physical structure of the city.

Rotterdam relies on mobility

Of all the major cities in the Netherlands, Rotterdam is the one most suited to meet the demands of modern mobility. This is due to its history. The city was

founded on trade, and through the centuries it flourished by virtue of trade. Its main economic success began at the beginning of the twentieth century, when the port shifted its focus to trans-shipment. When goods were offloaded from ships, they were no longer placed in warehouses or stores, but were immediately loaded onto smaller vessels, barges or other forms of transport. This innovation brought about an unparalleled upsurge in port activities and income.
After the Second World War, a similar development emerged as more goods began to be transported across land. Quite unintentionally, the bombing of the city in 1940 meant that the city centre could be reconstructed in a manner appropriate to the demands of modern motorized traffic. A grid of broad avenues was created, to which a ring of motorways around the city was added in the 1960s. The expansion of the port from the old city to the open sea went hand in hand with the gradual development of a varied infrastructure of almost 'un-Dutch' proportions. Along the axes of mobility, Rotterdam grew to become a major logistic centre and the 'gateway to Europe'. The waterways, bridges, dikes, canals, avenues and through roads became the lifeblood of an extended urbanized region.
Rotterdam is an ideal city for the car. The centre is readily traversable and a good place for 'street cruising', while the through routes offer spectacular views and experiences. On a somewhat more modest scale, the city provides space for other modes of transport, such as the bicycle, skates, water taxis, the new experimental 'people mover' or the trusty old tram. Rotterdam's affection for its own infrastructure is evident from the picture postcards in the souvenir shops, showing views of the port, bridges, viaducts, tunnels and traffic junctions.

A new challenge

Despite the heroic efforts of the port and the presence of such modern traffic systems, the economic growth of Rotterdam and the region went into something of a decline in the 1990s. The rugged world of logistics and transport could not compete with the sophisticated world of information and services which were thriving in other parts of the country and beyond. Nevertheless, Rotterdam did manage to attract new economic activities in such areas as culture, leisure, entertainment and retailing. Further transformations will be essential to secure the future of the city and the region. Rotterdam must take full advantage of its competitive strengths. Besides its spatial dimensions and an almost 'American' mentality in offering so many opportunities, Rotterdam's selling points include its physical infrastructure and a planning tradition which has revolved around movement and the urban dynamic for the past hundred years. The challenge for the twenty-first century will be to build upon that tradition and to 're-invent' Rotterdam, possibly by strengthening the relationship between mobility, urban development and the urban culture. There are many dimensions to this challenge. Some are examined in this book, which offers an impression of Rotterdam from the perspective of mobility. The city also presents an excellent opportunity to study and demonstrate how mobility can influence urban development. No matter how one chooses to approach the relationship, mobility remains an important and extremely topical social issue and incorporates a significant interdisciplinary and 'transdisciplinary' dimension.

VISIONARY PLANS

The great and significant changes that Rotterdam's traffic structure has undergone in the last century can often be attributed to the visionary ideas and determination of individuals. The city's history can be read as a series of lifeworks.

Dolf Broekhuizen

WATER PROJECT

PORT CONSTRUCTION

CITY ON THE RIVER

KOP VAN ZUID

METRO

COOLSINGEL

RUIT OM ROTTERDAM

CITY EXPANSION PLAN

STRUCTURAL PLAN

URBAN RENEWAL

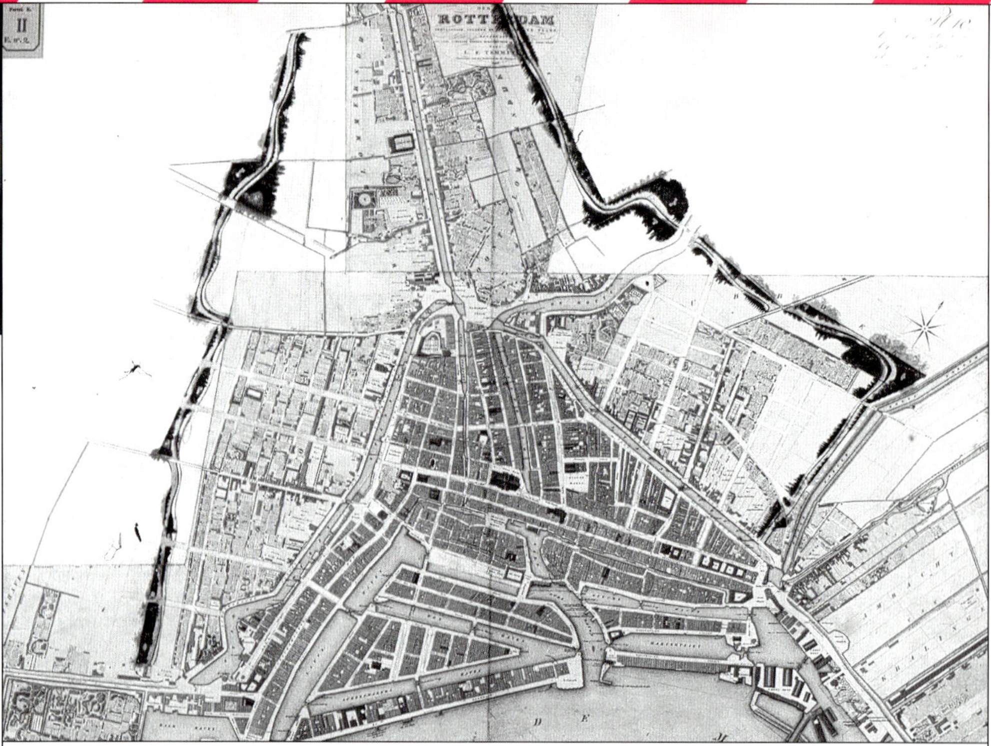

W.N. Rose

1854

When he was appointed as Rotterdam's city architect in 1839, Willem Nicolaas Rose found a city with numerous problems in its public works. Contagious diseases were endemic to the slum areas, the port wharves had exceeded capacity, and the bodily wastes of a growing number of inhabitants were being dumped into the city canals. To escape the stench, crowds and disease, more and more businesses were opting for premises outside the city. The Water Project (1854) that Rose designed in response provided the city with a high-grade system of water purification and offered direction for the city's expansion, in the form of a system of streets and a route for a singel, or ring-canal promenade. The canal promenade, which formed the new city boundary, was designed as a prominent residential environment, with trees, ponds and footpaths. Mansions, town houses and middle-class residences were located here. The city would soon expand beyond these new city limits, however. The Westersingel, Diergaardesingel, Boezemsingel, Crooswijksesingel and Noordsingel became a green belt within the city.

WATER PROJECT

G.J. de Jongh

1879–1910

During the period in which G.J. de Jongh was the chief of Rotterdam's Department of Public Works, the port city underwent explosive growth. Between 1879 and 1910 the size of the municipal area, the number of shipments passing through the port and the city's population all tripled. The character of the port also changed: it evolved from a depot market into a port of transit docks. To address these developments, De Jongh was forced to abandon the enclosed city concept that Rose had followed for his ring-canal promenades. He established new docks outside the city triangle. On the left bank of the Maas, he planned the Rijnhaven and Maashaven docks as well as the first section of the Waalhaven. On the right bank, in a westerly direction, came the Parkhaven, St. Jobshaven and Schiehaven docks. The docks were provided with good access through new railway lines. Dockworkers settled near the docklands, in new residential areas in Zuid – south of the river – and in the west of the city.

PORT CONSTRUCTION

A.C. Burgdorffer

1913

Under the leadership of Burgdorffer, director of Public Works from 1910 to 1922, Rotterdam acquired a new city heart, which in its representativeness was in tune with the scale and the allure of the new docks. Burgdorffer integrated the relocation of the city centre on the Coolsingel with the numerous incidental traffic breakthroughs, filled-in waterways and slum clearance that had been undertaken around 1900 within the scope of urban improvements and rising mobility. He wanted to replace the existing city centre around the St. Laurenskerk with a new and grander centre on what had once been the western edge of the city. Starting in 1909 the impoverished neighbourhoods of the Zandstraatkwartier were cleared and the Coolvest was filled in. In succession, a new city hall, a post office and the Bijenkorf department store appeared along the Coolsingel, followed around 1940 by a new Stock Exchange building and the HBU high-rise. The interventions did create a representative boulevard, but the traffic snarl-ups on the north side, at the Hofplein and the Delftse Poort, and on the south side at the Van Hogendorpplein remained.

COOLSINGEL

W.G. Witteveen

1928

In his capacity as head of the Urban Development department, Witteveen presented an expansion plan in 1928, in which the existing city and its future expansions were viewed as a whole. A continuous greenbelt structure and a system of radial streets served to unify the patchwork of old villages, residential neighbourhoods, industrial areas and the city centre. Green wedges, consisting of public gardens and parks, formed the backdrop for the construction of parkways, an idea, adopted from the United States, to situate motorways in the midst of areas of vegetation. This brought nature and provincial traffic deep within the city, which was divided into districts. Although the Overall Expansion Plan was not granted the force of law, it did determine the direction of spatial planning in Rotterdam in the 1930s.

CITY EXPANSION PLAN

C. van Traa

1946

The destruction of Rotterdam's city centre in May 1940 provided an unexpected opportunity to solve a number of traffic problems. In the Reconstruction Structural Plan, presented by engineer Van Traa to the Rotterdam authorities in 1946, the traffic structure forms the foundation of the future development of the city centre. Traffic was given space, thanks to a system of thoroughfares for through traffic right across the city. This design served as the guideline for the reconstruction of the city for quite a long time. The efficient system of north-south and east-west connections branched off in the centre into a system of pedestrian shopping streets, of which the Lijnbaan is a prominent result. A monumental fountain on the Hofplein square marked the starting point of the Coolsingel as the central city axis, continuing to the Maas river. This 'window on the river' created a spatial connection between the city centre and the river, which had been lost through the exodus of dock activity toward the North Sea.

STRUCTURAL PLAN

G. Plantema

1959–1968

After the Second World War, the new residential and employment areas in Zuid and the increase in regional automobile traffic started to exert increasing pressure on the existing permanent river crossings in Rotterdam – the Maas Tunnel and the Willems Bridge-Koninginne Bridge route. G. Plantema, director of Public Works, was a great proponent of resolving these bottlenecks by building a new public transport tunnel under the Maas. In his view, it behoved a port city to opt for tunnels. The Netherlands' first metro, built under Plantema's direction between 1959 and 1968, ran between the Central Station and Station Zuidplein railway stations. The metro stops evolved into urban transport hubs. One example is Station Zuidplein, where transfer facilities for city and regional bus services, tram and metro were combined with shopping and sport facilities for the entire district.

METRO

A.G. Quack

1957–1973

The *Ruit om Rotterdam* ('Rotterdam Diamond') is part of the redevelopment of the national highways in the 1950s and '60s. A rhomboid network of two- and four-lane intersection-free motorways and two new river crossings (the Van Brienenoord Bridge and the Benelux Tunnel) led regional traffic not through the city, but around it. The design of the ring was developed between 1957 and 1973, through the cooperation of national and city authorities: The national Directorate-General of Public Works and Water Management (RWS) bore primary responsibility for the national highway network, and the Rotterdam's Department of Public Works was engaged because of its knowledge of the local situation. A.G. Quack, chief engineer and director of the RWS, was the driving force behind the completion of the Ruit. The RWS engineers considered the Ruit – in line with Rotterdam's reputation for progress and innovation – a suitable testing ground for new forms of traffic flows, as evidenced by the Kleinpolderplein flyovers, which looked futuristic at the time.

RUIT OM ROTTERDAM

0134104665353

J.G. van der Ploeg

1974

The 1970s saw a fierce reaction from the population of Rotterdam to such large-scale interventions as the construction of the Ruit and the implications of the Base Plan. The planned razing of nineteenth-century neighbourhoods to accommodate motorway construction, the city's expansion and the clearing of bad neighbourhoods aroused a great deal of resistance among residents. They were organized within their districts and demanded more say in these matters. City authorities were receptive. Following J.G. van der Ploeg's appointment as alderman for urban development in 1974, residents were given a majority interest in the project groups that managed urban renewal operations. Drastic demolitions made way for renovations and 'building for the neighbourhood'. Small-scale solutions and the search for a welcoming and cosy housing environment were given priority. Attention shifted from regional motorways to the laying of pedestrian- and bicycle-friendly, traffic-restricted residential streets with benches, zigzag routes and planters. The Coolsingel itself was sheltered from automobile traffic and dotted with terraces, pavilions and public gardens.

URBAN RENEWAL

GEORGE BROWN COLLEGE
CASA LOMA LIBRARY LEARNING COMMONS

Riek Bakker

1991

For almost a century the *Kop van Zuid* (the 'South Bank of the Maas') was reserved for docks and sprawling working-class neighbourhoods. This changed at the end of the twentieth century with the transformation of the Kop van Zuid. This ambitious project traded the concept of the Structural Plan's 'window on the river' (1946) for the 'leap across the river'. The old city triangle on the right bank, where the pre-eminent administrative, business and recreational functions had been concentrated, shifted south to the other side of the Maas. The construction of such high-grade infrastructure as the Erasmus Bridge (1995) and the Wilhelminaplein metro station improved access to the area and made redevelopment possible. The determination and effort of Riek Bakker, then director of the Department of Urban Development, saw to it that the urban planning framework designed by Teun Koolhaas for the Kop van Zuid (1987), became a reality starting in the 1990s.

KOP VAN ZUID

Joost Schrijnen

2001

In the 1990s, Joost Schrijnen, as director of Rotterdam's Department for Urban Planning, Housing and Traffic (dS+V), focused on the Maas as the pre-eminent public space in the city. The Maas is no longer seen as a transport axis for merchant shipping but as an attractive location for housing and recreation. To achieve this, contact between the city and river should be rendered as uninterrupted as possible. On the map of the 'City on the river', plans have been drawn, in various stages of development, of the places where Rotterdam can build residential, employment and recreational areas along the riverfront. These are sites where a reallocation of dockland functions is necessary, as well as a revitalization of existing residential areas without denying the place's rich history as a substantive component within the new design. With this attempt to create a synthesis among incidental interventions, Schrijnen creates a model for the denser construction the city needs.

CITY ON THE RIVER

Peter Dreier PLACE MATTE

Aldo Rossi L'ARCHITET

LA

Geert Mak HOE GOD VERDV

LIVING IN THE FAS

Siegfried Giedions MECHANIZATIO

SENSUOUS CRITER

Auke van der Woud LEGE LAND

Richard Sennet THE CORROSION

Francine Houben THE VIEW F

Wies Sanders NICHT HINAUSL

LA CITTÀ MUOVERE

Towards a phenomenology of the space of flows

Luuk Boelens

RS
URA DELLA CITTÀ
CITTA ANALOGA
EEN UIT JORWERD
LANE
TAKES COMMAN
FOR HIGHWAY DE
TOURBANISM
OF CHARACTER
ROM THE ROAD
HNEN

Place-specific thinking

In the second half of the last century, Aldo Rossi's *L'Architettura della Città* (1966) focused interest on the term 'archetype' once again. In this work, in a counterpoint to a functional approach, the city is primarily considered as architecture. Architecture is not so much viewed as a construction, but rather as a creation that cannot be viewed independently of the life of the citizens or the society in which it stands. This was developed further in Rossi's idea of the analogue city – *la città analoga* – a city that is composed of pure, elementary building types (the archetypes), referring to shared memories and analogies (the collective memory) and closely connected to an urban form that is based on a specific urban geography and topography (the morphology). The 'genius loci' is akin to this. As a counterbalance to modern technology and the maelstrom of global developments, which uproots people, alienates them from one another and makes them restless, the meaning of the 'place', with its own unique character, history and identity, has been given special importance. This place is supposed to regenerate people's reason and appetite for living, which is more than simply residing somewhere; it also inspires an intuitive solidarity with the place and the quality of its social and spatial environment. It is the task of architecture, urbanism and planning to articulate and convincingly express that meaning.

Since then, this call to arms has been taken up within the architectural and urban planning disciplines, but also far beyond. Consider, for example, Auke van der Woud's Lege Land (1987), his doctoral thesis on spatial order in the Netherlands from 1798 to 1848, Geert Mak's chronicle, *Hoe God verdween uit Jorwerd* (1996, published in English as *Jorwerd: The Death of the Village in Late Twentieth-Century Europe*, trans. Ann Kelland, 2000), or the recent expostulations on political economics and planning around the theme of Peter Dreier's *Place Matters* (2001). This rise in popularity is also due to far-reaching globalization by networks independent of borders and worldwide in scope, which privileges the specific place's uniqueness, exceptionality and identity in re-establishing its importance. No matter how real and valuable that effort might be, however, the fact that this is only half the reality is often forgotten. And often it does not even reflect the latest innovations, for besides the analogue there is also now a digital reality. Besides the symbolic, architectural and cultural meaning of the urban centres, there is also an urban field which has developed as a social, economic and spatial reality. And alongside the geography and topology of places, there is also a new morphology of flows, with its own order, its own specific reality and potential for development. This does not mean that we can throw the entire tradition of the *città analoga* and the meaning of 'place' out with the bathwater. Rather it calls for a determined effort to develop a new typology, in parallel with a new approach, from the angle of the complementary reality that has been created by the world of flows and networks.

Mobile thinking

Fortunately this conclusion is gaining more and more support. From its origins in the mobility studies of E.J. Marey and Frank B. Gilbreth (1910 –

1920), it later gained greater standing in architectural theory in Siegfried Giedion's *Mechanization Takes Command* (1948), and it was translated into urban planning theory with Lynch and Appleyard's *Sensuous Criteria for Highway Design* (1958). Almost half a century later, this issue has once again been taken up by Francine Houben, Professor of Architecture and specialist in mobility aesthetics, in her inaugural lecture: *A Room with a View* (2002). However, there is a noticeable revival in the design of infrastructure and mobility in other areas. In the context of the project 'Wegen naar de Toekomst' ('Roads to the Future'), the Dutch Ministry of Transport, Public Works and Water Management carried out research into 'the lovely road' and in 2002 it launched a competition for 'Living in the Fast Lane'. Four years have passed since Ashok Bhalotra's design for the HSL-Zuid (High-Speed Line railway, southern section) was nominated as a *Grand Projet*, two years since Jo Coenen's design for the A12 was granted similar status, and only last year the OMA design for the Adertienboulevard was named a 'key project' for the Zuidvleugel (the 'South Wing' of the Randstad, the densely populated urban agglomeration in the west of the Netherlands). Infra-bodies, infra-ecologies, motorway landscapes, inhabited bridges and noise barriers now fascinate countless architects. And as if that's not enough, the jewel in the crown is that the theme of the first International Architecture Biennale in Rotterdam is the relationship between architecture and mobility.

What has struck me repeatedly in this summary is that the disciplines associated with place and geography and those associated with movement and flows do indeed communicate with each other – appearances to the contrary notwithstanding – but they hardly arrive at a new definition of the mobile reality. The architects remain trapped in their familiar architectural métier and continue to be primarily interested in designing the place or the construction, although this is now perceived at greater speed. Conversely, the civil engineers and logistics experts stick to their own typology (merge in transit, cross-docking, just-in-time delivery, one-stop shopping) and their own *modi mobili* (individual-collective, fast-slow, monomodal-multimodal), which seem to have little to do with the thinking in terms of spatial dynamism mentioned above. All the spatial thinking in terms of movement and mobility aesthetics thus remains tied to the geography of place and locale; albeit in sequence now, like a series of cartoon images. The reference to the collective memory and historic analogies per transport corridor (like the Louis Couperus route, the Erasmus route, the Rembrandt route, the Zuiderzee route, mentioned in Houben, 2002) is apposite here. And lastly, the design of infrastructure or places along these lines remains imprisoned in the genius loci, as if it were something that must imbue meaning, character and identity in an ever-greyer world of mobility: 'Look! I live in the "Fast Lane" now, travelling along that lovely road!' The meaning of places and their specific position in the network, relatively independent of their geographical context and as components of a borderless and world-encompassing system of mobility, remains underexposed.

Without entertaining the pretension of being exhaustive or indeed of being in a position to arrive at a conclusive answer, I shall strive here to redress these omissions in our thinking about mobility. As a counterbalance to the archetype and the *genius loci*, I want to tackle the 'mobitype' and the *genius fluvii*. By choosing these two paths, it may be possible to make substantive progress in the fields of analysis, signification and design of the diffuse world of flows, the 'space of flows'.

The drive-in

The drive-in is the prototype, the elementary spatial form that has arisen from the most individual mode of mechanical transport, namely the car. Originally this automobile promised us unprecedented freedom, adventure and renewal. That tale actually began with the laying of the first railways, but only really took off with the introduction of the car and the construction of the first motorways. 'Liberated from points and rails,' wrote Paul Morand in 1941, 'the horizon spreads out before us anew, free and alone at the wheel of the machine. We can again make use of the empty spaces between our cities.' And in the last century this took place to the full. An urban sprawl of suburbs containing the drive-in (home, cinema, shopping mall, restaurant, motel, etc.) marks the unconditional surrender to individual mobility's promise of freedom. The terraced house and the single-family house are the watered-down polder variant of this. The cons are now familiar enough as well: noise and environmental pollution, damage to the landscape and ecology, congestion, morning, afternoon and evening stress, rising oil prices, geopolitical rivalries, an epidemic of violence and death, as well as burgeoning social isolation. This does not detract from the further evolution of the drive-in in new guises. The designs in the context of MVRDV's 'motorway landscape' and VDVDV's design for the Mandela Bridge in Arnhem could, for example, be seen as the modern-day variants of the drive-in. We can certainly no longer manage without the car, despite it now being patently obvious that the car does not provide us the freedom and bliss that was promised.

The mobitype

The mobitype can be defined as an archetype, a model that can be traced back to a primitive form, an original example or the disposition toward a materialized movement or a mode of mobility. It does not say much about the actual mode of transport, instead saying more about the relationship between transport and traffic on the one hand and the spatial infill of the conceptual thinking around it on the other, 'for the betterment of society' as it is so elegantly put. This relationship essentially began at the start of the nineteenth century, when the industrial revolution spurred a massive acceleration and expansion of mobility, so that in the long run it became an independent force which has its own conditioning effects on the spatial layout. Prior to this, traffic and transport were more dependent on the speed of wind and horse, and lines of infrastructure mirrored geographical features. In the recent history of the autonomous relationship between space and movement (and the more serious theorization about it), a number of basic forms of the topography of flows have developed almost by stealth. These can be classified according to those mobitypes which are more or less established, but which can be clearly profiled with respect to the flows and their specific position within them (the 'static types') and those types which literally and figuratively also generate their own dynamics and are thus an integral part of the flow itself (the 'mobile types'). The distinction between 'in stasis' and 'in motion' is almost no longer applicable.

The caravan

The caravan offers an escape clause out of this deadlock. After all, this mobitype combines the letting-one's-hair-down escapism and the exciting pleasure of travel with the security, privacy and safety of home. After all, in the caravan we find the literal and figurative fusion of home and mobility. Ever since the definitive domestication of society somewhere around the time of the mercantilist revolution, this kind of mobile home had been exclusively reserved for Romanies, market traders, circus artists, migrants and the like. With the growing demand for recreation and tourism, however, it has also taken off in other sectors of society. Between 1880 and 1910, a tour in a horse-drawn replica of a gypsy wagon was a favourite vacation in England. And with the start of automobile mass production around 1920, the so-called 'motor home' also took over the American highways. Since then it has also drawn the attention of pioneering architects. Buckminster Fuller designed the Dymaxion House (the name stands for 'dynamic/maximum/ions') as early as 1928, Jean Prouvé started to experiment with rapidly dismantled and transportable houses in 1937, and Carl Koch designed the Acron House, which was specially suited for transport by truck, in 1945. Alongside these examples, beginning in the 1950s, first Yona Friedman and later Constant Nieuwenhuis, as well as the Archigram group of architects, also designed large-scale three-dimensional space-frames structures, into which living, working and amenities units can be 'plugged', temporarily or permanently. Both variants are currently the subject of renewed interest, though sometimes in a different form or in a different way. The first is intended not only for use as a camper for a growing population of retiring baby-boomers, but also in the form of mobile offices – big vans equipped with fax, cellular phone, laptop and TV – or as vans for mobile kitchens or education. The second takes not so much the form of Archigram's and Friedman's hardware solutions, but more that of the 'orgware' variant, as time-share constructions which answer the increasing demand for shared housing, in other words tourism or 'expat living' in different places throughout the year.

It is also possible to make a distinction based on plane, line or point. This distinction is related to the kind of mobility (individual or collective) and the exchange points between these movements and/or with the specific place in question (station, port, exit, terminal, etc.). After all, personal transport often spreads itself diffusely across a large area and therefore in mobitypes which manifest themselves in a plane. Collective transport, by contrast, always follows a fixed line or timetable and thus results in a linear typology. The exchange between this collective and individual transport (between train and car, for example) or between this flow and destination always occurs at a point, however, and thus leads to a point typology.
These two angles of approach result in the following matrix, in which six (2 x 3) mobitypes can be distinguished. In fact there is a confrontation here between the basic principles of movement (individual and collective, as well as their transfer machines) and the primitive types of society or lifestyle (in this case more settled or more nomadic forms of life) with a direct spatial

effect, which can be typified as a basic form of a more mobility-oriented spatial strategy. This is explored further in the boxes. These examples clearly include sections of the aforementioned strategies, but this also highlights the limited reach of current thinking in terms of the aesthetics of mobility.

	PLANE	LINE	POINT
STATIC	Drive-in	Strip	Junction
DYNAMIC	Caravan	Cruise	Cocoon

The strip

The 'strip', the third spatial prototype of the mobile society, is in part the result of increasing mobility. According to Robert Venturi and Denise Scott Brown, the strip is almost entirely composed of graphic signs. Due to increasing speed, the clarity of the Cartesian urban space is no longer sufficient, and additional signs are needed in order to guide the motorist with clarity: public signs for the sake of order and traffic flow, private signs as an enticement to consume. Moving through Las Vegas is also a movement through a massively extended textural landscape of signs and symbols. In fact this goes back to Otto Wagner, Walter Curt Behrendt and Hendrik Pieter Berlage, though these designers had a greater appreciation for the change in architecture. Because of increasing speeds it is no longer possible to perceive the individual family house, only the collective housing block. A more natural and recreational variant of this is the parkway. The 'high-profile' locations with businesses plainly visible from the road, or even Houben's 'room with a view', are in a sense related to this as well. Nevertheless, influenced by TV channel-hopping, computer-serving and multi-tasking, a new visual culture is developing for which big, fixed signs seen from a distance are no longer enough. One beckoning alternative for the waning attraction of the strip is 'The Freemont Street Experience' which was recently built in downtown Las Vegas as a big commercial entertainment landscape with a daily *son et lumière* using more than 2 million little lights burning up 540,000 watts of power. Access is now by trolleybus and on foot from a parking facility for 1,500 cars.

The *genius fluvii*

Because they are fraught with hesitation, and often still highly inadequate, we are at best seeing the preliminary experiments in the field of the more stationary mobitypes, such as the drive-in, strip and junction. Regular institutions are tentatively issuing commissions for initial studies, such as 'Living in the Fast Lane', the design of the A12 or the design for Zurich's Hauptbahnhof railway station. With respect to the more diffuse and dynamic mobitypes such as the caravan, the cruise and the cocoon, however, this is not the case, by a long way. The development of these mobitypes is still left to artists (often considered bizarre and harmless) or to the transport and knowledge sectors themselves. That is a shame, because these mobitypes are not merely an expression of the new demands that are evolving while on the move, but they also present new opportunities for the better use and organization of time and space. Indeed, these more diffuse and dynamic mobitypes turn mobility itself into a 'destination', in which the distinction between flow and place is in fact completely absent. As such, they therefore also furnish a dynamic upgrade for the architectural, urban planning and traffic planning toolbox, in which spatial layout, planning and design do not exclusively count as a spatial activity, but must also be seen as a temporary and temporally cyclical activity.

It is only in this sense that thinking in terms of flows and mobility aesthetics forms a welcome replenishment of the classic archetypology. In this manner, mobitypes can be an expressive vessel for the world of flows (the space of flows) as an independent force with its specific spatial and logistical conditions, alongside the familiar world of places (the space of places) with which we have long been familiar. They thus satisfy a need for or give expression to the spatial context of a specific kind of lifestyle, that of the *homo movens*. The drive-in and the caravan typify individual mobility, the strip and cruise the collective, while the junction and the cocoon provide the more hybrid interaction between these flows, regardless of the distinct modalities.

The cruise

Like the drive-in and caravan, this strip is made mobile in the cruise: travel itself is the destination.

The modern cruise liner is three times bigger than the Titanic and offers at least as much entertainment as any amusement park; not only for tourists, but also for the leisure, shopping, trade-fair and corporate markets. There are even plans in the offing for ocean liners which can hold an entire village of almost 10,000 people, including a church, cafés, sports fields, TV broadcasting facilities, theatres, shops, work and conference spaces. Other transport modalities still trail far behind. The rudimentary precursors to such developments, in the first part of the last century, could be seen in railway travel, the 'Pullman' coach and the aeroplane. These days, however, terms such as cost reduction, punctuality targets, operational efficiency and transport capacity predominate. Yet we find ourselves sitting more often and for longer periods of time than ever before in our modes of transport. We are also seeing a growing demand to turn travel time into quality time. New developments are underway in aviation to come up with interior designs that are flexible and adaptive to demands or circumstances. At the International Architecture Biennale in Rotterdam, a copy of Niels Norman's 'geo-bus' will be driving around, a bus furnished like a nature area and making a tour of natural areas. And lastly, following the lead of Vito Acconci, the HSL-Zuid design studio has already made a case for the high-speed train as a place of sojourn; whether as a space for meditation and reading, or a work and/or meeting space, or as a space for art.

However, it should be emphasized that this new typology cannot be read as a new dichotomy in society; as if the poor and the bumpkins would be well served by archetypical designs, and the wealthy and the worldly by mobitypical spatial interventions. In *The Corrosion of Character* (1998), Richard Sennet convincingly argued that, in our society of information technology and telecommunications, the private and public spheres and those of home, work, travel and recreation are increasingly starting to intermingle. This is also the case with the spheres of flows and places. Even the most hardened globalist and networker has a need for places that are replete with identity and well established, just as the most hardened bumpkin is starting to travel more and more often. In the Netherlands, people travel on average more than 35 kilometres a day, and three to four times a year they travel a much greater distance.

The junction

Unlike the examples mentioned above, the junction is a mobitype that not so much facilitates mobility as provides interconnections for it, mono- or multimodally. It therefore not only imbues special value to the spot in question, but also to the network itself. Nevertheless, one junction is not the same as another, and as a type it can already claim an intriguing history. In *De stad en de haven* ('The city and the port', 1996), for example, Han Meyer describes the evolution of a depot-market port, by way of a transit-shipping and industrial port, into a regionwide distribution port within the network city. In the wonderful essay 'Railway Stations and Local Communities in Japan' (2001), Kuniaki Ito and Masatsugu Chiba outline the evolution of a railway station into an identity-imbuing interface between a local community and the rest of the world, and finally into a hub almost inextricably integrated into the urban fabric. In *The Drive-in, the Supermarket and the Transformation of Commercial Space in Los Angeles* (1999), Richard Longstreth describes the evolution of the petrol station with a single pump, by way of a super-service automobile station and drive-in supermarket, into a mega shopping, leisure and factory-outlet centre. And finally, in this field we also find the noteworthy developments of the aviation hubs from a landing strip in the meadow, by way of airfield into an 'Airport City' or perhaps a polynuclear urban airport area. In all these examples we recognize not just the increasing scale of the junction, but also an ever more diffuse interaction with its surroundings, immediate and wider. It demands an adapted strategy that cuts through all the levels of scale, in which logistics and culture, economy and sociology, and private and public are all essential elements.

This does nothing to detract from the utility of an analytical distinction between the archetype and the mobitype, all the more because the latter deserves extra attention in an increasingly mobile network society. This holds especially for the application of these mobitypes to specific forms of network use and organization. In the same way that thinking and designing in terms of the *città analoga* presumed not merely knowledge of the archetypes but also a grasp of the genius loci, thinking and designing in the context of the *città muovere* presumes not only knowledge of the mobitypes but also of the *genius fluvii*, in other words the specific conditions and needs of the flows, at different times and moments, as well as the networks, arrangements and coalitions involved. The place itself also acquires a different meaning. Everyone will readily acknowledge that the network conditions of Schiphol Airport are different to those of the suburban Duivendrecht railway and metro station, the Eemshaven port, or the exit for Ruyven Delfgauw from the A13 motorway. This is also the case with the network conditions of motorways, waterways, railway lines, flows of capital or the World Wide Web. This involves other key parties, with other interests and motives. However, this has not yet produced a detailed strategy for tackling these different flows, or a strategy for how to design them or render them spatially. This is still often left to expediency and chance, instead of being informed by a well-considered and balanced approach. Nevertheless, it is now almost universally accepted that our society is evolving at an accelerated pace into a society in which not just places but also flows and networks are relevant. However, this has not yet elicited an adequate response from designers and architects, because besides a 'dynamization' of our fixed ideas about time and place, what is required is a renewed and humane design of networks and flows, as well as a reorientation of the way in which design can fulfil a supportive role.

The cocoon

Lastly, the cocoon is a mobitype that, just like the junction, can be characterized as an interface or intermediary, but it is allied to the evolving information technology society and not to physical flows. Here it no longer actually matters whether someone is standing still or mobile. Using the new – and now universally mobile – visual, aural and mechanical devices (tele-vision, tele-phone, tele-computing, etc.), people can stay in contact with the entire world remotely. The cocoon or capsule facilitates this condition. Think, for example, of spaces into which people withdraw, such as a telephone box or in a reading or video booth in a library, train or boat. It is also possible to insulate yourself from the environment with devices such as video glasses, a portable CD-player or headphones. The cocoon is a piece of equipment on its way to becoming an integral part of a lifestyle. This view can be traced back to Kisho Kurokawa's 'Capsule Declaration' and his Nitto factory in Yamagata (1964), the Hawaii Dreamland recreation centre (1967) and the Nagakin Capsule Tower in Tokyo (1972). Nevertheless, these are all fixed buildings, where people can use a small space for a brief respite, just like the famous capsule hotel. We are also now seeing more mobile variants of the cocoon, such as the Head Cocoon (2000) and the Cocoon Chair (2000) by the artist Jennie Pineus, or the flexible work cocoon designed by students at the Tilburg Academy for Architecture and Urban Planning. The mobile variant of the cyber-helmet, fitted with three-dimensional video, laptop and cellular phone, was exhibited as early as 1999 at the Frankfurt auto show.

This article is in part based on an introduction to a discussion about the cultural heritage of the twentieth century for UNESCO that was held in Paris in October 2001; an introduction to the special issue on 'Mobitypes' of the periodical *Stedebouw en Ruimtelijke Ordening* ('Urbanism and Spatial Planning') 2001; the essay 'Tourbanism' for the former Rijksplanologische Dienst (Dutch Spatial Planning Agency) from 2001, as well as the lecture, 'Nicht hinauslehnen', given by Wies Sanders at the Mobi-Pret ('Mobi-Fun') symposium hosted by Holland Railconsult in Utrecht in August 2002.

3 ZONES

ROTTERDAM PORTRAITS

Bas van Toledo

ie Bergwerff [37] Mr. Van Twist [48] **VAN**

RESS 'This vehicle is only for work. With all that bloody stuff, tools and asterboard, it's impossible to do it on foot. We do lots of jobs together d we have a good laugh in the van. You have to, because people wadays are in such a rush and so stressed out on the road and they're ally aggressive too. And that means you get pretty mad on the road well!'

yan Bakker [16] **SCOOTER**

EJUDICE 'My father bought this scooter for me. Pretty cool, don't you ink? I've souped up the engine. My mum's sent me to get some butter the market. I've had this scooter for six months now, and it's really ly for getting to school. What I've noticed? Lots of people are ejudiced against people on scooters, because they're supposed to speed freaks.'

efano [19] **QUAD**

TTING NOTICED 'I was looking for something special, something cool, mething that other people don't have. Everybody's got a scooter eady, and I can get noticed with the quad. I've just been to school and heading home now, and with my quad it's easy and quick to get rough all the traffic. It's great to have people looking at me when I'm t. At the weekend I go cross-country.'

ohammed Belal [21] Mouslim Elaissali [23] **CAR**

VOURS FOR FRIENDS 'I'm just back from football. This morning a team-ate picked me up here, and I forgot to switch off my headlamps. alled my friend Mohammed and he came straight from Zuid. I've been ing in Rotterdam for three years now, and we're from the same city in orocco. We work at night and a car is a must, because there isn't any blic transport.'

F. Kerkhof [64] **BIKE**

NCE PARTY 'I've been unfit to work for a couple of years now. I don't ve a car and for me the bike is the quickest and best mode of trans-rt. I'm out looking for a hall for a country and western dance party xt month. I cycle every day, seeking out unknown little streets, old ighbourhoods and the peace and quiet of churchyards. That is how scape from the anonymity and how I get to enjoy the beauty of tterdam.'

RET
Slinge
Lift
Slinge

Tickets
Enkele reis en Retour
Tickets
Enkele reis en Retour
Tickets
Enkele reis en Retour
Tickets
Enkele reis en Retour

ssan Ismal [22] PEDESTRIAN

MPED 'I'm off to pick up my girlfriend from college. She's 21 and she's 't me, and I'm going to ask her if she'll come back home. I live close to e Zuidplein, but I hardly ever use the metro. I don't have a car, though. s another ten minutes' walk to the college. Wish me luck!'

menico Sessink [23] Kevin van der Ree [12] SPECIAL TRAIN FOR FOOTBALL SUPPORTERS

ST MATCH 'We come from the east part of Rotterdam, and the football ain is the quickest way to get to the Kuip stadium. This is the first time at Kevin has been to a Feyenoord match, because he's always been an ax supporter. At my first match 13 years ago I was surrounded by vay supporters in front of the stadium and I had to run for my life.'

m Mahie [18] PEDESTRIAN

HOPPING 'I've been waiting for my boyfriend for a while. He's coming train from Schiedam but he's late. It's not nice waiting at the station, ecause all kinds of strange people approach you. I came here with the am. We're supposed to go shopping in the city. It's not such a big ing for me, but he wanted to come to the city.'

arloes van Rossen [25] METRO

RE-DODGING 'I come from Deventer and I've been living in Rotterdam for year. I work as a care assistant for addicts, and the weird thing is that I ever ever pay for a metro ticket. I've only been caught for fare-dodging ice, so I've easily covered the costs of the fine. It's great that there's a w metro line now, because then I can get to my in-laws in Schiedam sier.'

Wout van Dijk [46] **CAR**

SHEIK ARMANI 'This car used to belong to Armani, a Saudi sheik. He was to blame for the oil crisis in 1973. This car was his wife's, for doing the shopping at their holiday home in Switzerland. It was already a beautiful car, but I still had to do a lot to it. I bought it two years ago to go on nice trips at weekends.'

Irene Kremer [55] Ruud Poelstra [50] **WATER TAXI**

SENTIMENTAL JOURNEY 'We're colleagues and I'm showing Ruud where my roots are. We're staying in Hotel New York and a trip with the water taxi is a must. We've had a long, nostalgic weekend in Rotterdam, and later we're heading to the Hook of Holland to look through the dirty windscreen at the big ships on the Nieuwe Waterweg with a bag of chips and mayonnaise, just like the old days.'

Water taxi captain **WATER TAXI**

A JOB ON THE SIDE 'Being captain on the water taxi is like a little sideline. Normally I work as captain of a tugboat in the Rotterdam docks, but for about eight days each month I'm a skipper on the water taxi. We work in a kind of partnership with a few skippers. It's really busy in the summer and at weekends. It's great, I do it just for fun, and it's not really tiring.'

Rob den Hartog [44] **PIPER PRIVATE PLANE**

NO TRAFFIC JAMS 'I've been flying since 1977, but I've only been a flying instructor for the last two years. I do it on my free days. What do I think is so nice about flying? I never get stuck in a traffic jam, I feel the freedom of the skies, it's incredibly peaceful, and looking down on Rotterdam is like looking at a Lilliputian city, with its beautiful bridges and the Nieuwe Waterweg shipping lane.'

P.P
Coca-Cola

Daniël de Reus [17] **LORRY**

NTERNSHIP 'I'm studying Transport and Logistics, and I'm currently doing an internship. I'm only the driver's mate for a food supplier because I'm too young to drive myself. It's pretty good fun, but I don't want to pursue it. The Port of Rotterdam must be great, and I'd like to work there later.'

Ricardo Zweden [43] **BIKE**

FLAT TYRE 'A postman needs a specially reinforced bike. I still have to buy a new bike every 18 months. On top of that, on average, I have a flat tyre every week. I've been a postman for 17 years already, including a number of years with the post van, but that wasn't for me. I'm happy to be in the open air again, with my own beat and familiar residents.'

Shaun Jeffery - England [31] **CAR**

PARKING ILLEGALLY 'This bass guitar is a present for my girlfriend in Rotterdam. I work in the docks on a contract and I brought over my own car. As an Englishman I can earn more working in the Netherlands than in England, and then I can save up for a trip to Australia in the near future. I'd better get a move on before the police arrive, because I'm parked on the pavement.'

Hisham Raji [22] **SCOOTER**

DELIVERING PIZZAS 'We've been open for just four months. To start with I did the deliveries by scooter myself, but now all my time is spent baking pizzas. I've had a few delivery guys, but they drove like madmen. That period's behind me now, and I'm a bit calmer. The scooter is quicker than the car for doing deliveries, because you can get through the busy traffic.'

Mr. Broekhuizen [45] **RIVER-VESSEL**

IN A HURRY 'I've been doing this job for 25 years and sailing is my lifeblood. Without a barge I wouldn't have an income. I travel between Germany and Delft transporting gravel. Now and again, if I have time, I go into Rotterdam. The bridges and locks in Rotterdam function well, but I'm in a hurry and I really have to get on. We still have to get through the city and later on the bridges won't be raised.'

11.9

Mark van de Aardweg [20] **SKATES**

SPEED BEATS BALANCE 'With my friends I want to do as much skating as I can in as many possible places in the Netherlands as I can. I didn't even finish school because I was too busy. We're not from Rotterdam, but Rotterdam is tops because of its street-spots in concrete and steel. Our slogan is "speed beats balance". The faster you go, the more balance you have, but you also hit the ground harder. Sometimes people clap if we do fancy tricks, and that's cool!'

Lenn van Beek [27] **SKATEBOARD**

URBAN HOVERCRAFT 'I have my own shop for custom-made clothing: Lucky Lenn. Every morning I go to work on my skateboard. It gives me a completely new perspective on the street. Along the way I've got all kinds of spots to do jumps and I know all the kerbs where I can try out new tricks. It's a fun game. With my "urban hovercraft" I can easily slalom through the traffic and then I feel really free.'

Margot van Ewijk [43] **BIKE**

ENJOYMENT 'The bike is a brilliant form of transport, and that's without even considering the environment. I use the bike every day, I'm mobile and I can quietly enjoy the little bits of nature in the city. It's a shame that there's a lot of broken glass on the streets and often it takes a long time before cycle paths are repaired. Now I have to go to Zuid to pick up my paintings that were on loan.'

Mr. Schenkeveld [66] **THREE-WHEEL ELECTRIC SCOOTER**

OUT AND ABOUT 'The doctors don't know what it is. My legs sometimes give way and I'm overweight. I'm on a diet, and I'm hardly allowed to eat, drink or smoke. Without the three-wheel scooter I would be sitting at home looking out of the window every day. That would be alright if I could knit or bake, but I can't. Every day I get out and about for an hour or so. I get a breath of fresh air and do the shopping.'

RET

werken
wonen welzijn ondernemen
DE KERN
DE KERN
SUZUKI

Ruby Dominicus [48] **PEDESTRIAN**

ESUS WANTS YOU 'I've been standing here distributing folders for 18 years olders about the Gospel. Yes, Jesus will save us, and everyone should .now that and feel it. Sometimes I stand in Amsterdam or The Hague. 'm about to go shopping, because I need bread, greens and flowers. On Tuesdays I always go to the big market on the Blaak by metro.'

Nadjeska Jack [19] **TRAM**

HURCH ON SATURDAY 'I go to church in Crooswijk every Saturday morning or an hour. I've lived in the Netherlands for five years, and I was already a member of the Seventh Day Adventists in the Antilles. I haven't got a car and I've come by train from Barendrecht. Then I take tram 4 to Noord. feel really comfortable in the tram and it means I don't need a car.'

Mrs Sitaran [34] **CAR**

RREGULAR SHIFTS 'This little car is wonderful. I work irregular shifts, and in he evening I don't dare walk the streets. The St Francis Hospital is fairly emote and it doesn't feel safe. We're off to buy presents at the Zuidplein. My husband often does the day-to-day shopping by bike. We do the big shopping trips in this little car.'

Jacqueline de Maat [39] **BIKE**

SSENTIAL 'I've been living in Rotterdam for three years, and I've already had my bike stolen twice. Unfortunately in Rotterdam you have to watch out for your bike being stolen. But I can't do without it, because Rotterdam is big and you can get to know it quickly on the bike. I also have to take the children to school, and the car isn't very handy for that. Now I've got a long walk ahead of me to get back home.'

MOBILITY IS CENTURIES OF CITY BUILDING

Martin Guit
Harko Stolte

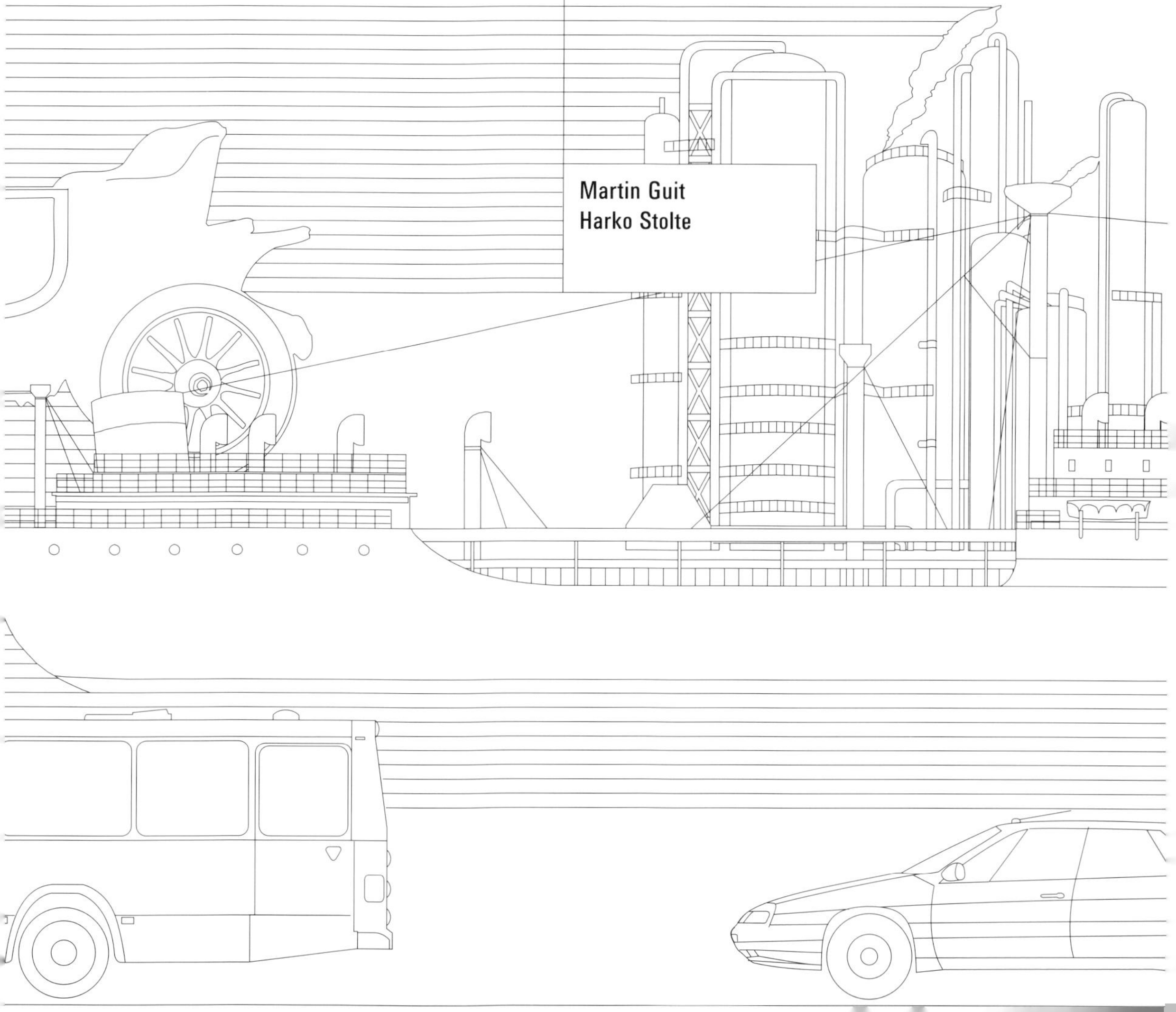

Infrastructure is the stage for the movement within a city, be it by water, road or rail. The infrastructure network, in its rich variety, is a dominant factor in the cityscape. The history of this infrastructure is inextricably linked to the development of mobility and urban development. The use of infrastructure changes over time. Infrastructure itself is also continually adapting to new developments. New means of transport are introduced, and flows of traffic are widened, redirected, branched off, merged, subdivided or stacked. Technological developments and social dynamics speed up [accelerate] this process. Since the structure of a city and of an infrastructure network evolves much more slowly than daily use and available technology, it is inevitable that the structures built are already outdated by the time they go into operation. Moreover, they often remain unchanged for centuries. In view of the rapid development of traffic, the gap between the unwieldy (infra)-structures of cities and the dynamics of use continues to widen. In this context it is relevant to study the relationships between mobility, infra-structure and urban structure and incorporate them in the planning. The conflict between the current mobility requirements and the historical mobility culture comes to the fore more and more frequently. Uncovering the topical relevance of the history of the physical infrastructure may serve to define the design of the future. Such a future will have to be based on insights into and knowledge of the past. Taking Rotterdam as its example, this essay describes how the infrastructure took shape during the urban development and what relevance it has for the city of today.

The history of the Rotterdam's physical infrastructure

The physical infrastructure of Rotterdam primarily took shape during periods in which the city was undergoing economic growth. In the first centuries of Rotterdam's history, transport was mainly on foot, and the range of movement seldom exceeded the distance people were able to walk in a day. In the sixteenth century the radius of action of the population expanded rapidly, for some even as far as the oceans. Industrialization, the construction of the railways and the increased scale of the shipping trade put a whole new range of destinations within reach for Rotterdam's nineteenth-century citizens. An even larger expansion of mobility took place during the twentieth century, due to the introduction of motorized traffic, aeroplanes and the acceleration of all sorts of means of transport. Today's individual range of movement has exploded, so that hardly any unknown places remain.

Routes in and out of Rotterdam: 1150–1500

The first interventions in the delta area where Rotterdam came into existence were aimed at defending the land against the water. Halfway through the twelfth century the first dike was built in the swampy delta and the reclamation of the hinterland began. Around 1300 the river Rotte was dammed, near the present Hoogstraat. Subsequently, the first houses could be built. The dam in the Rotte was the final piece in an extensive water-retaining structure intended to defend the hinterland against floods. On and behind the constructed dikes the 'dry' town continued to emerge. Around 1400 this settlement consisted of approximately one thousand houses.

Shipping, trade and industry were growing rapidly. For the protection of the still infant town against looters, two moats were dug – the Goudsevest and the Coolvest. Trade and shipping required new connections with the hinterland, and these were also dug. Thus emerged the Oude Haven ('Old Harbour'), the connection for shipping between the river Rotte and the river Maas, as well as the water connections to the Delftse Schie, Delft, The Hague, Leiden and Amsterdam. The first land connections with the hinterland ran in straight lines from the town to the surrounding villages. These quays, such as the Kruiskade, were the only passable routes through the swampy land.

The old routes to and from the town originated from the morphology of the landscape and were extremely practical in layout. A lot of the connections dating from that time still exist and retained their destination as transport axes throughout the centuries. The present-day city is arrayed around this old infrastructure. The dikes as routes remained visibly present in the city and proved capable of coping with the evolution of mobility through the centuries. The river Schie was not just an excavated shipping lane; the road leading from Delft to Rotterdam also ran along its bank. In the early twentieth century this road was diverted to the trajectory of what would later be the A13 motorway and the Stadhoudersweg, straight through the city expansion district of Blijdorp. Nevertheless the Schie is still one of the main routes to the heart of the city today, though the Schie has now been filled in to accommodate cars and trams.

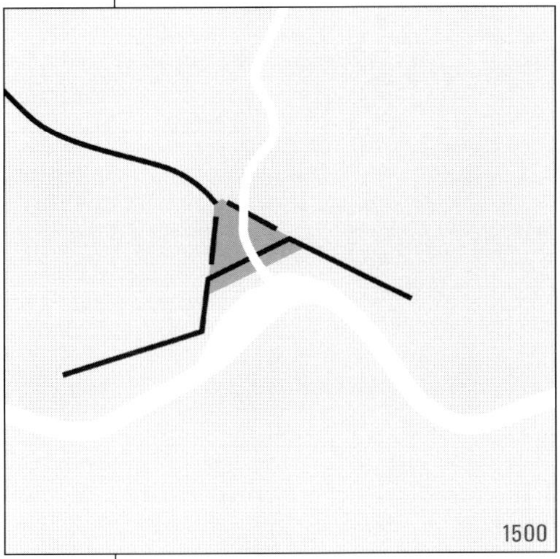

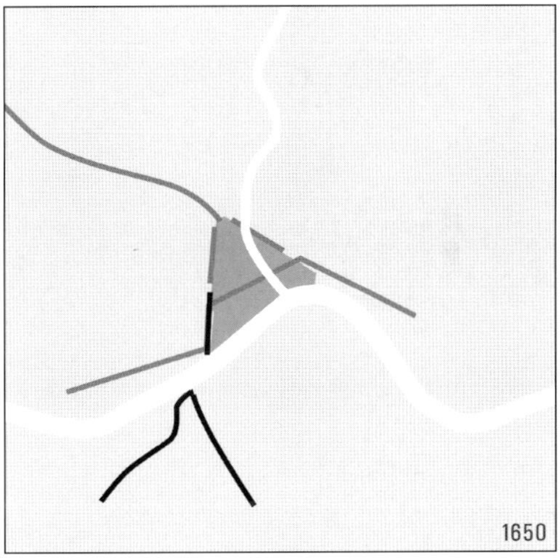

Rotterdam as a trading town: around 1600

At the end of the sixteenth century Antwerp fell into Spanish hands and many wealthy Flemings took refuge in the northern Netherlands. Rotterdam also profited from this migration and prospered during the Golden Age. The fact that the waterways to and from Dordrecht, Rotterdam's major competitor in those days, silted up was a godsend for Rotterdam. Rotterdam could expand unfettered. The town cultivated the Maas Delta. Urban expansion mainly took place in the area outside the dikes, so that trade and shipping literally came to occupy the centre of the town. Rotterdam really became a town of movements: transport and transhipment. Several major docks and quays date from this period, such as the Blaak, Leuvehaven and Haringvliet. Because the town was growing toward the river, the moats had to be extended as well. The Coolvest was dug through to the Maas. The 'Boompjes', on the banks of the Maas, was not only laid out for the protection of the town, but also as a promenade. The town was also graced by prominent buildings, such as the town hall on the Binnenrotte, right in the middle of the town centre.

Rotterdam owes some new connections with the hinterland in the south to the Golden Age. A route to Dordrecht ran via a ferry across the Maas to the village of Katendrecht, and there was a new connection to the islands of South Holland. The physical infrastructure in those days mainly consisted of docks, most of which are still to be found in the present-day city. Some docks were later filled in for traffic purposes, such as the Blaak. Both of the old connections to the hinterland to the south of the town can be found in the present-day city, namely as the Dordtsestraatweg and the Waalhavenweg.

Rotterdam and the railways: around 1850

In the early nineteenth century agriculture prospered greatly, and the age of industrialization and modern engineering also began. With the introduction of the railway and the switch from sailing boat to steamship, transport made a gigantic leap forward. At the same time mobility over land became more important than over water. However, the town had not expanded in two hundred years and had to contend with a huge overpopulation and the attendant hygiene problems. These circumstances had a great impact on the physical infrastructure of the town. The old infrastructure was adapted and new infrastructure was laid out.

Initially, the railway lines and stations were situated outside the old town. A line to The Hague and Amsterdam was constructed with a terminus on the north side, and a line to Utrecht with a terminus near the Maas to the east of the town. In order to solve the problems of poor hygiene and overpopulation, architect W.N. Rose instituted a Singelplan ('Ring-Canal Plan') for Rotterdam. Not only did this establish the foundation for a proper water system, but it also gave the population a chance to move out of the overpopulated 'City Triangle'. The new ring-canal structure simultaneously formed a new mobility structure, which still dominates the spatial structure of the modern city.

Metropolitan Rotterdam: until 1940

The opening of the Nieuwe Waterweg in 1886 was the prelude to an unprecedented increase in scale of the port. From now on the largest of the new sea-going vessels could put in at Rotterdam. The port's expansion was the focus of attention during this period. The waterway and the recent railway connections allowed Rotterdam to develop as a modern port.

The expansion of transhipment, the larger market and the agricultural crisis in the provinces of Zeeland and Brabant induced many people from the countryside to move to Rotterdam and try their luck there.

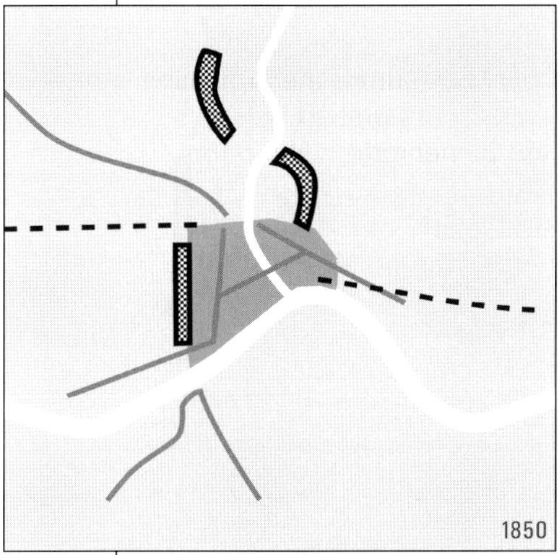

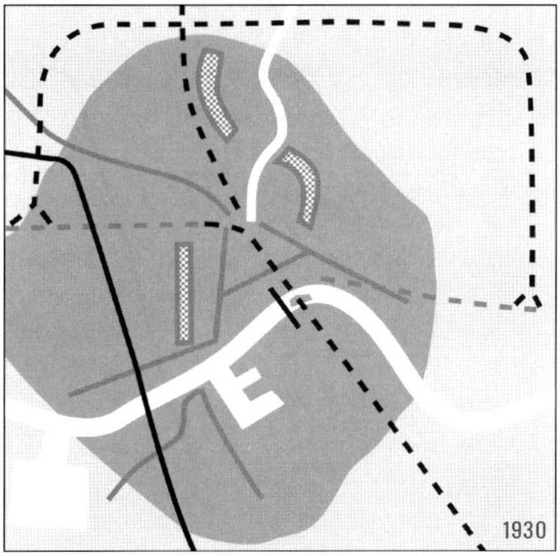

At the end of the nineteenth century the resulting population increase and the subsequent expansion of the city were already significantly underway. In 1875 Rotterdam had 130,000 inhabitants; 50 years later that figure had reached 600,000. Initially, the port expanded on the left bank of the Maas, outside the limits of the seventeenth-century town. The Rijnhaven and Maashaven accommodated the new steamers. The new Willemsbrug provided access from the old town to the new port quarter south of the river. In addition, the growing population had to be able to get about in the poverty-stricken and polluted port quarter. New transport systems were introduced. The bicycle and the (horse-drawn) tram made their entry, soon followed by the car. Many old waterways were filled in to accommodate these new flows of traffic, e.g. old moats including the Coolvest and Goudsevest, which were incorporated into modern Rotterdam as boulevards. In addition, the railway network was further expanded. An additional connection to The Hague via Pijnakker and Zoetermeer (the Hofplein railway line) was established. Another new regional line was the steam-tram connection to the island of Voorne-Putten. The greatest physical impact, however, came from the construction of the railway bridge across the Maas, creating a direct railway connection to the south of the country. This route left its mark in the old city centre. The railway track cut through the old town on a long viaduct, following the course of the Rotte, to the new railway lift bridge across the Maas ('de Hef'). The Binnenrotte had to be filled in for this intervention. In 1877 the elevated railway to Dordrecht was a fact. The Binnenrotte lost its position as a pleasant area in the city centre and the town hall was also relocated. The role of the Binnenrotte was taken over by the filled-in Coolvest. Along the Coolsingel a series of buildings was built in the 1920s and '30s: the City Hall, Post Office and Stock Exchange. Only since the opening of the railway tunnel a decade ago has there been a glimmer of hope that the filled-up Binnenrotte will grow in urban and local significance in the future.

From the 1930s onwards the car was to take an ever more prominent place in the cityscape. In the old impenetrable city centre, openings were broken through to create space for all the flows of traffic in and through the city. The Meent and the widening of the Noordblaak and Zuidblaak are examples of this. The first motorway near Rotterdam dates from the 1930s, and connected the city with The Hague and Amsterdam. Shortly before the Second World War, construction began on the Maastunnel. This became the new link that was to direct automobile traffic from Amsterdam and The Hague to the south of the country alongside, instead of through, the city centre. In addition, in the north of the city the Rotterdamse Schie river was filled in to make a connection between the new motorway and the Maastunnel.

Rotterdam and the post-war Reconstruction: after 1940

The bombardment at the beginning of the Second World War, on 10 May 1940, obliterated virtually all the buildings in the Rotterdam city centre. What survived was the infrastructure survived – streets, routes and squares. Once the debris had been cleared, the structure was still recognizable, and it was never far from the minds of the urban planners. Nevertheless, the Reconstruction did not aim to rebuild the pre-war city, but rather create a modern city centre. An efficient way of handling traffic was the main concern. The devastation provided an unexpected opportunity to adapt and correct the infrastructure. This resulted, for instance, in making new, large east-west connections. One of them was breaking through the Westblaak as an extension of the Blaak, which had been filled in with war debris. Two prominent north-south routes were also laid out. The first route ran from the Hofplein, which was shifted a little from its pre-war position, via the Coolsingel to the renewed and re-routed Schiedamsedijk. The second route was only partially completed, with the new Willemsbrug and Mariniersweg.
The network of railway lines across the city had already been modernized before the bombing, resulting in a direct link between the railway lines to The Hague and Utrecht. The old railway line on the east side, already discontinued prior to 1940, obtained a prominent, but completely different traffic-related role in the Reconstruction Plan. A new dam and dike structure was built along the Maas, topped by a panoramic car boulevard, from the Westzeedijk via the Boompjes to the Maasboulevard. The route developed into a major approach road of the city, from the motorway to the city centre, with a view of the city skyline.
The relationship between infrastructure and the underlying landscape has gradually faded in the twentieth century. New engineering techniques make it possible to build infrastructure on practically any foundation. Entirely new directions and flows emerged in the network of the city. First it was only the railway and tram lines, such as the rural Groene Kruisweg and national railway lines; national motorways followed. The new routes in and around the city form a link between the urban and the rural network. Both the railway lines and the motorways were constructed as a ring around the city. They have since been incorporated in the expanding city.

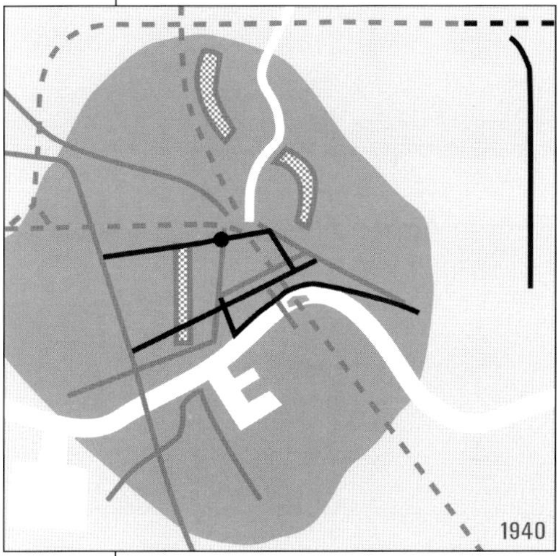

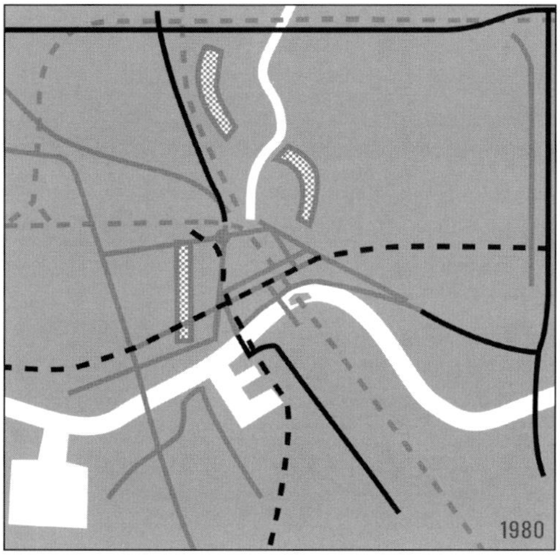

Rotterdam and the welfare state: since the sixties

After the war, new housing projects were not built in the city centre, but in the new suburbs bordering on the city. The old peat polders (Alexander, Ommoord) were developed, just as a number of areas south of the river (Pendrecht and Zuidwijk). Although all these new residential districts had their own amenities, they still largely depended on the city centre. People lived outside the old city, but for work, recreation and facilities the residents continued to rely on the central city. Good connections between the suburbs and the city centre were crucial. This resulted in a new increase in the scale of traffic. In the seventies the motorway system around the city (the *Ruit*, or 'Diamond', named for its a rhomboid pattern) was completed. Both of the north-south routes of the Ruit have since been doubled in size. This motorway system had a great impact on the existing infrastructure in the city. Existing routes, such as the Schiekade and the Schieweg, were transformed into high-traffic approach routes for cars. Elsewhere in the city new urban routes were created, such as the Vaanweg, which directly connects the Zuidplein with the motorway. Just like road traffic, public transport made a quantum leap with the building of the metro system. It was laid out in the form of an autonomous cross with a north-south and an east-west route through the city and was later extended to the surrounding residential areas of Spijkenisse, Capelle, Schiedam and Vlaardingen.
In the twentieth century, connections were laid out which transform urban structures from various periods into a new urban structure within the mobility of the present-day city. Such connections are not coincidental, and in a number of cases they fit directly into the physical structure of the city.
By adding these links new possibilities are created for the further spatial and programmatic development of the city. The present city axis, from the Hofplein, via the Coolsingel, to the Kop van Zuid, is an example. The development of this axis started with the filling-in of the Coolvest and its transformation into the Coolsingel, which was by then within the city limits

due to the first nineteenth-century urban expansion toward the west. In the Reconstruction Plan for the modern city, the Coolsingel was included in a larger network of urban infrastructure. This link was made by 'straightening' the Hofplein and extending the Schiedamsedijk, without affecting the Coolsingel as a 'special place' with an important recreational function.
With the construction of the Erasmus Bridge, this urban structure was once again incorporated in a larger mobility network of the city. The new bridge became the link between the old, changing docklands and the historic city.

Rotterdam: a stratified network

The physical infrastructure of Rotterdam is the result of a development process spanning centuries. Layer by layer, the city grew and expanded, and outdated parts were transformed. Infrastructure and mobility developed along with the city, sometimes following, sometimes leading the way. In present-day Rotterdam, the infrastructure is historically stratified, which contributes to the legibility and identity of the city. At a time when new, often drastic transformations are in the offing, an awareness of this historical stratification is crucial, particularly because of the 'cultural value' of the infrastructure as a point of recognition and identity bearer of the city. An insight into its historical growth is a useful tool in the design assignment for innovation and transformation.
In the early stages of its development Rotterdam was still connected to the surrounding land by direct routes. The morphology of the landscape largely determined this. As a result of technological developments the impact of this morphology steadily declined as centuries passed. After the dismantling of the defensive works of the city, space was literally and figuratively created for the enjoyment of movement: the promenade and the city boulevard defined the distinguished appearance of the city. The optimal and efficient traffic machinery grew more and more dominant over the condition of the soil, the structure of the landscape and the city itself. Railways, motorways, metro lines and main city routes illustrate this.
With the completion of a number of connecting links the network of the city was made even more complete: breaking the Meent through provided a better east-west street in the city centre, the Erasmus bridge extended the city axis to Rotterdam-Zuid. Such links also created new spatial and programmatic possibilities. A number of places in the city were thus rediscovered and brought into prominence.
The adaptation of the physical infrastructures to the modern mobility requirements will continue to be a permanent design task in the developing city. The original meaning and function of these spaces in the city are important aspects in this task. Through the centuries mobility has formed the structure of the city, and it will continue to do so. On the other hand, the urban structure has a great impact on the mobility culture of a city. Historical research into the meaning of infrastructure is still in its infancy, and defining the topical relevance of that history has hardly been started yet.

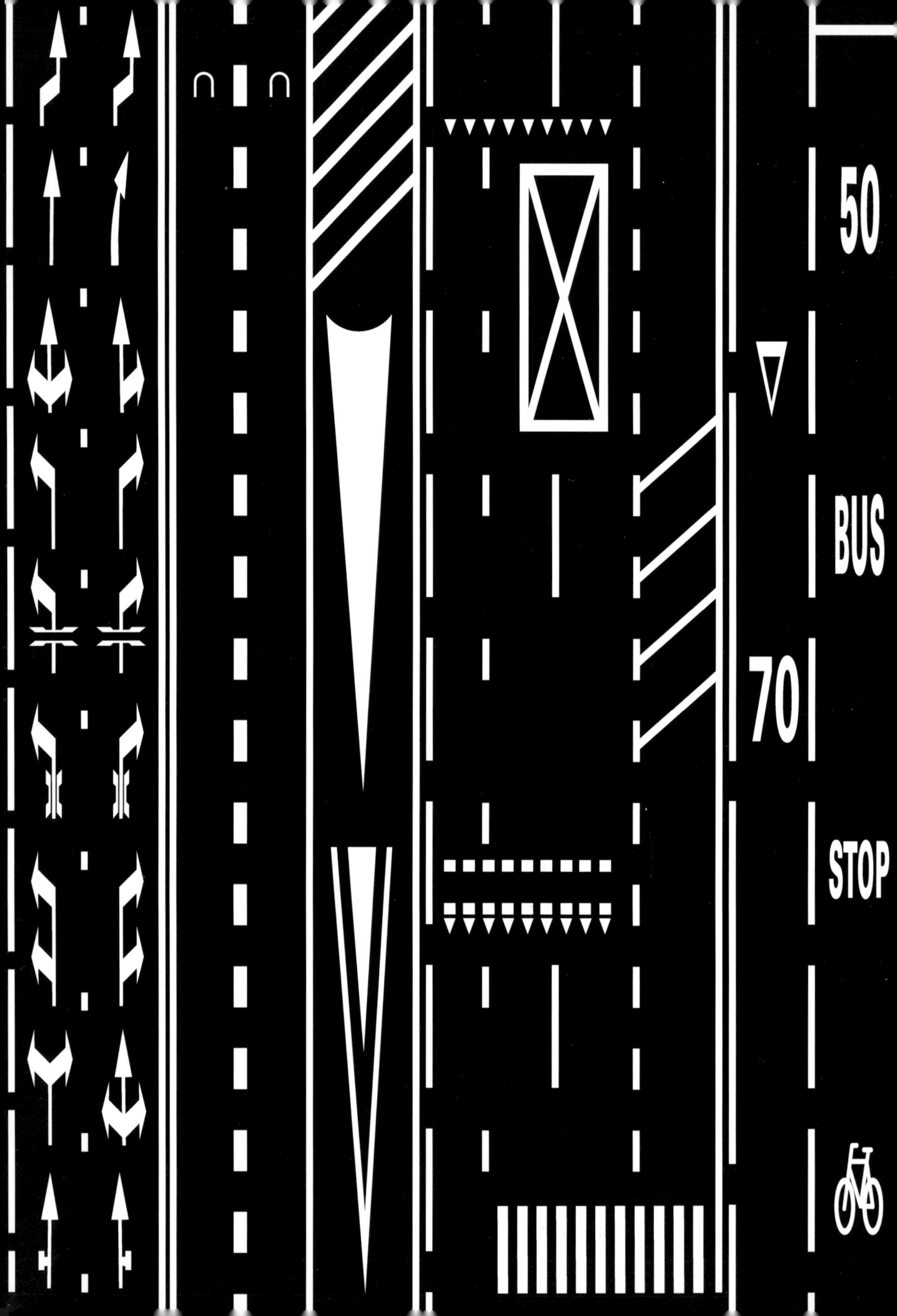
50
BUS
70
STOP

LEXICON OF MOBILITY

Minke Themans

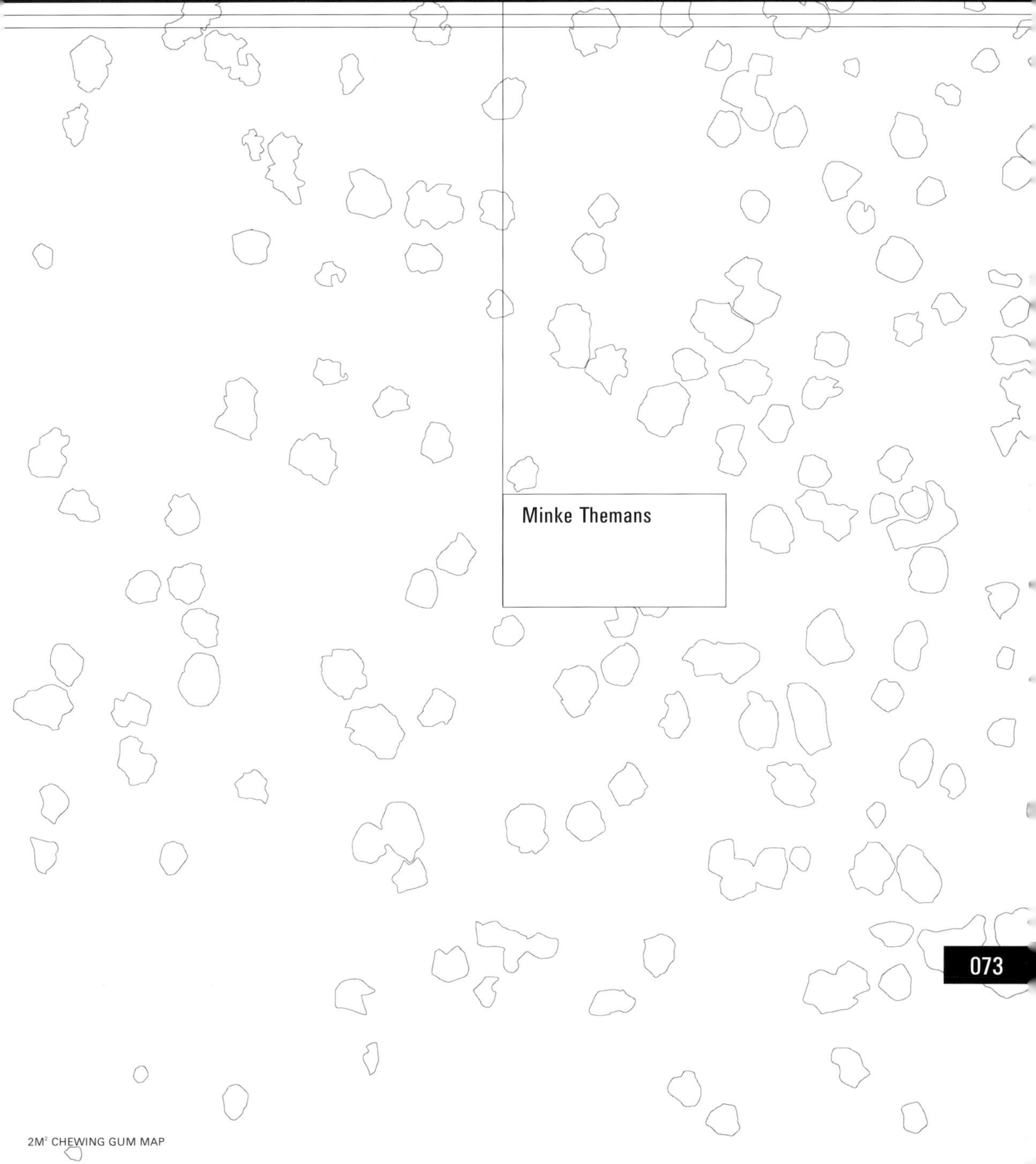

2M² CHEWING GUM MAP

Schieweg

Maaskade

Abraham Kuyperlaan

Abraham Kuyperlaan

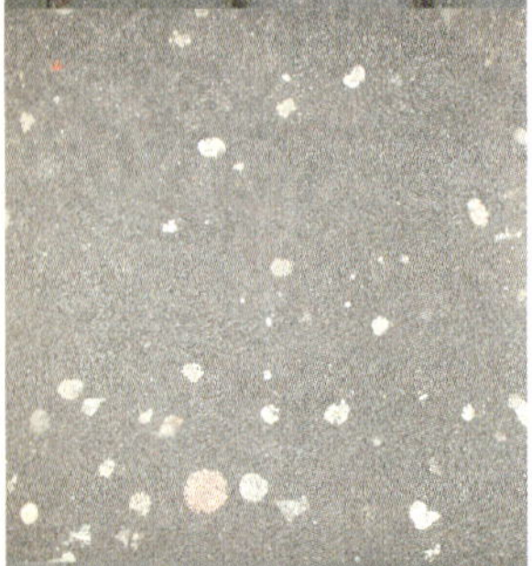
Schiekade

Claes de Vrieselaan

Zuidplein

Beurstraverse

Abraham Kuyperlaan

Station Zuidplein

Dreef

Voorburgstraat

Meent

Geertsemastraat

Dresselhuysstraat

Station Zuidplein

Abraham Kuyperlaan

Teilingerstraat

Entrepotstraat

Dresselhuysstraat

Pannekoekstraat

Abraham Kuyperlaan

Noorderhavenkade

Provenierssingel

Abraham Kuyperlaan

Centraal Station

Robert Fruinstraat

Centraal Station

Korte Hoogstraat

Beurstraverse

Beurs

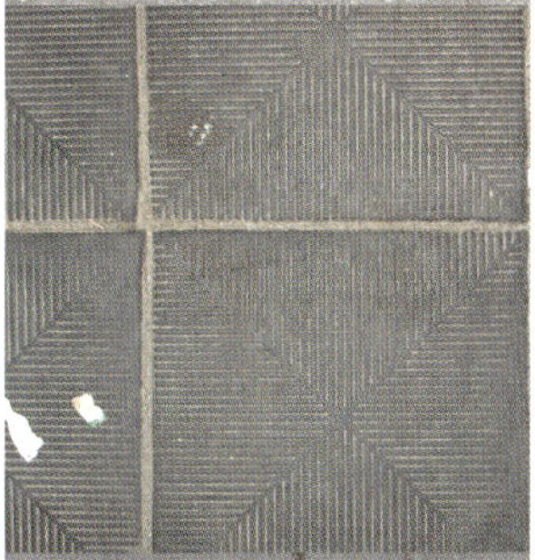

Station Zuidplein

Dokter de Visserstraat

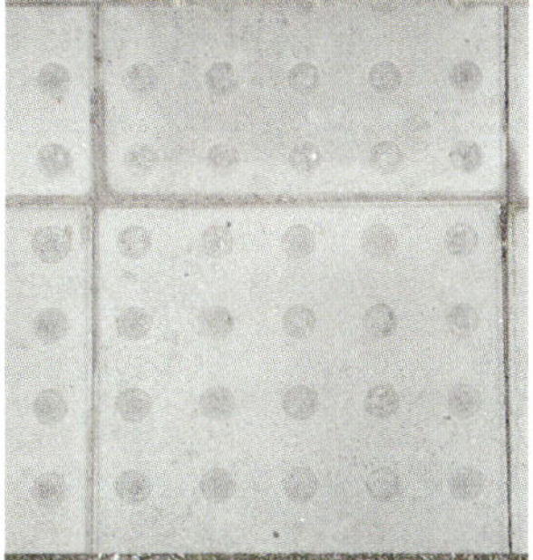

De Savornin Lohmanlaan

Beurstraverse

Station Noord

Robert Fruinstraat

Bergweg

West Kruiskade

Meent

Entrepotstraat

De Savornin Lohmanlaan

VERBETERD BLOKVERBAND

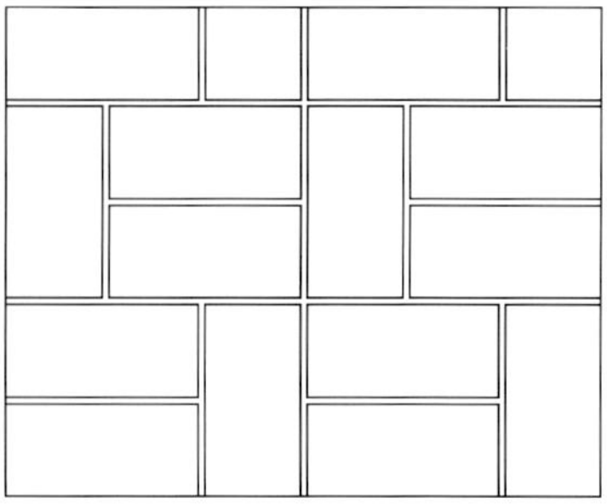

HALFSTEENSVERBAND

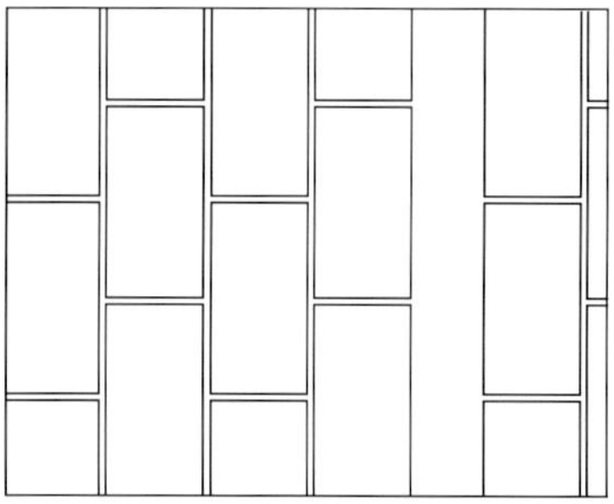

FANTASIEVERBAND

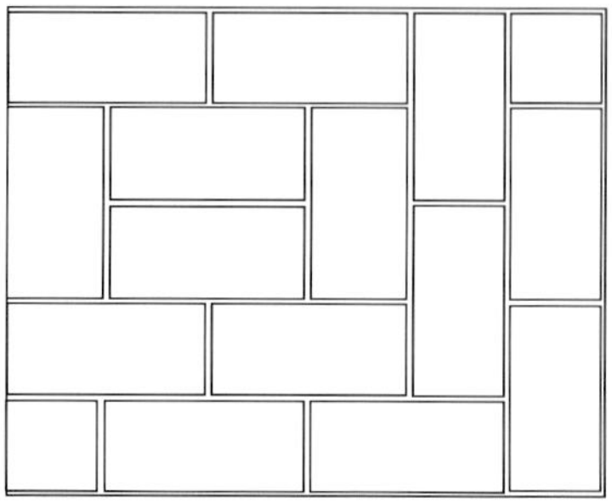

BLOKVERBAND MET TUSSENLAAG

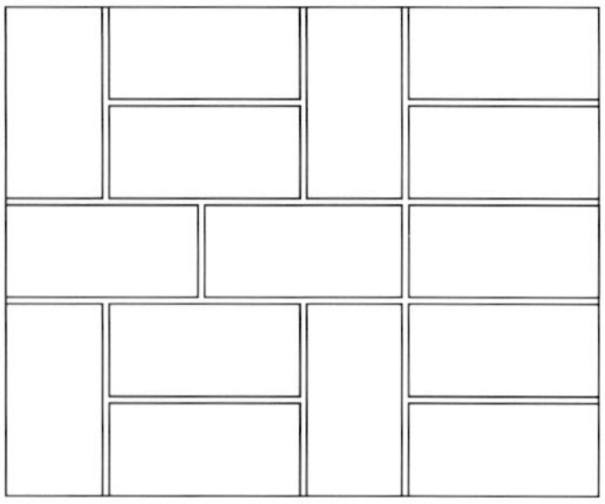

KEPERVERBAND

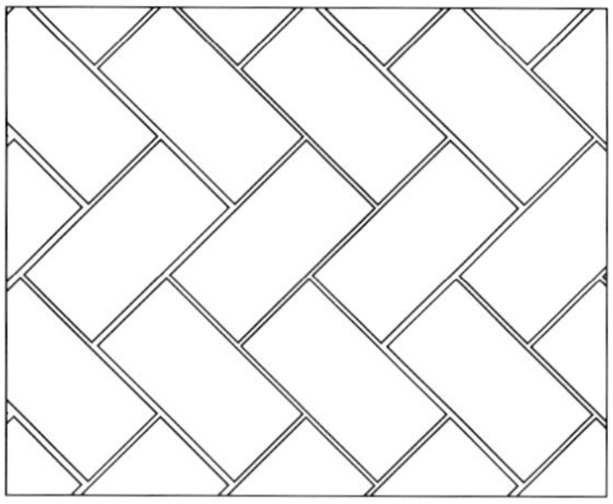

HALFSTEENSVERBAND

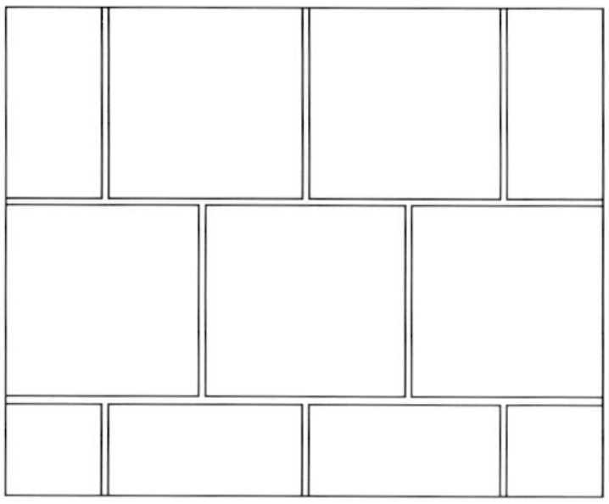

BLOKVERBAND

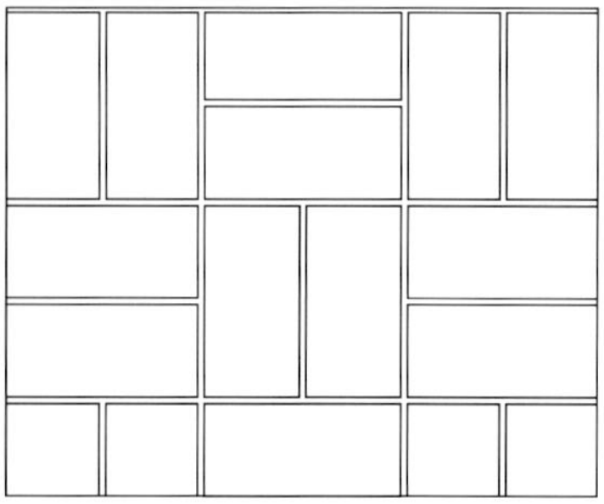

ELLEBOOGVERBAND

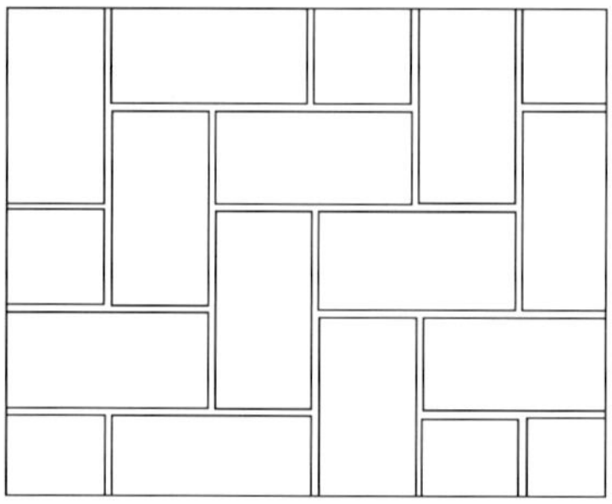

DIAGONAAL BLOKVERBAND

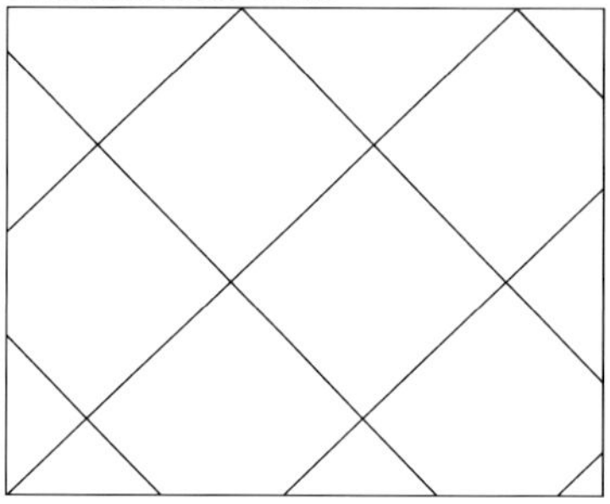

BLOKVERBAND

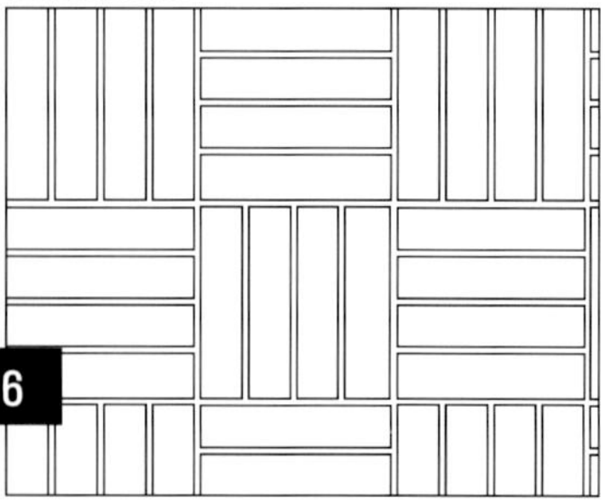

ELLEBOOGVERBAND

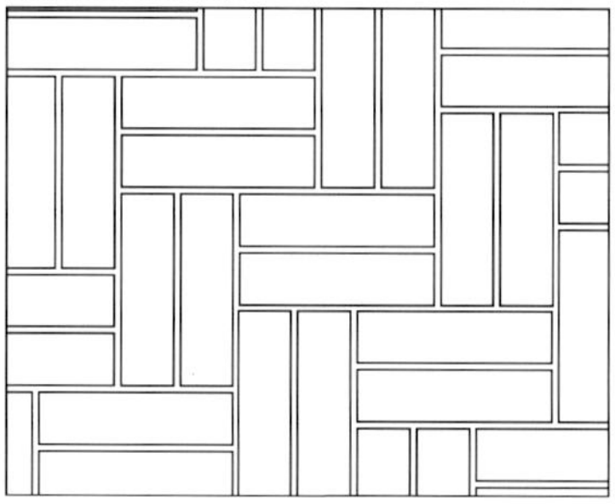

FANTASIEVERBAND

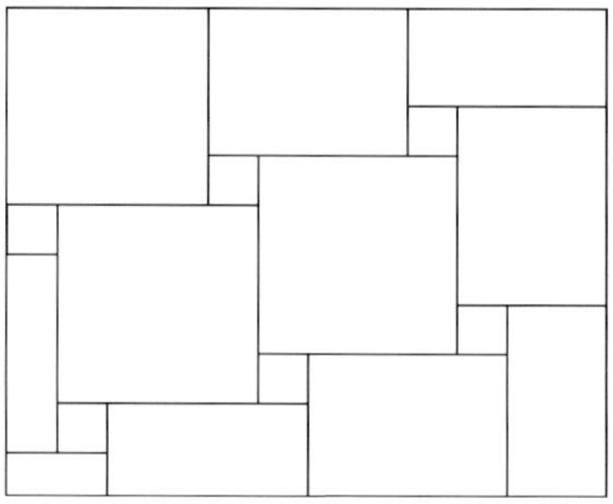

0 metre

46 metre

27 metre

1 metre

56 metre

0 metre

0 metre

19 metre

25 metre

61 metre

0 metre

39 metre

18 metre

5 metre

0 metre

55 metre

25 metre

8 metre

21 metre

0 metre

40 metre

79 metre

10 metre

9 metre

22 metre
0 metre
23 metre
25 metre
4 metre
6 metre
43 metre
10 metre
12 metre
13 metre
64 metre
72 metre
9 metre
64 metre
10 metre
0 metre
11 metre
8 metre

Rotterdam 001

Rotterdam 002

Rotterdam 003

Rotterdam 004

Rotterdam 005

Rotterdam 006

Rotterdam 007

Rotterdam 008

Rotterdam 009

Rotterdam 010

Rotterdam 011

Rotterdam 012

Rotterdam 013

Rotterdam 014

Rotterdam 015

Rotterdam 016

Rotterdam 017

Rotterdam 018

Rotterdam 019

Rotterdam 020

Rotterdam 021

Rotterdam 022

Rotterdam 023

Rotterdam 024

Rotterdam 031

Rotterdam 032

Rotterdam 033

Rotterdam 034

Rotterdam 035

Rotterdam 036

Rotterdam 037

Rotterdam 038

Rotterdam 039

Rotterdam 040

Rotterdam 041

Rotterdam 042

Rotterdam 043

Rotterdam 044

Rotterdam 045

Rotterdam 046

Rotterdam 047

Rotterdam 048

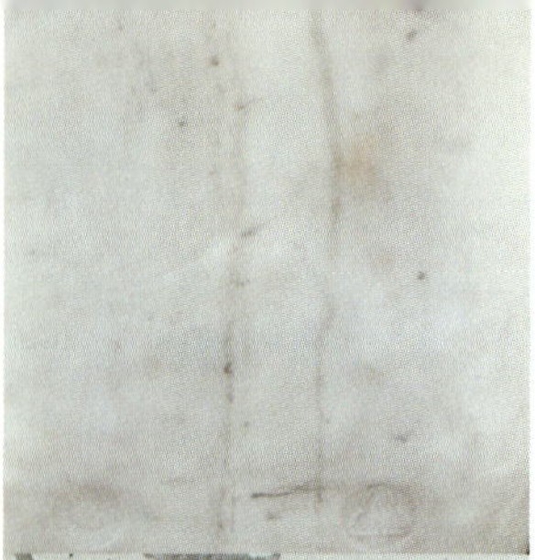
plastic-bucket white

lamppost white

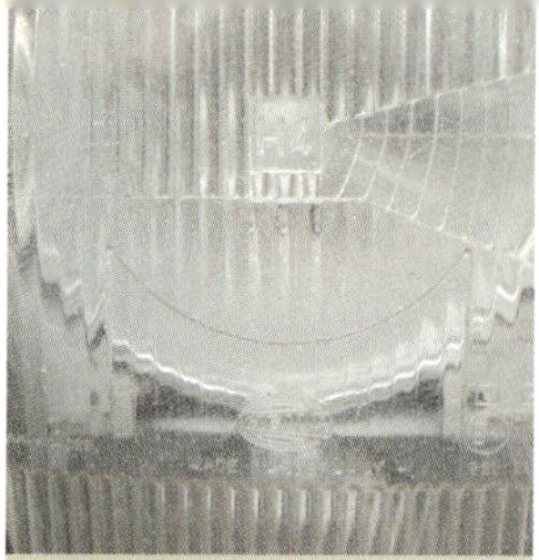
headlight white

bubble-wrap white

concrete paint off-white

Trespa sliding-panel off-whie

ambulance yellow

parking-bollard yellow

manhole-cover brown

shredded wood brown

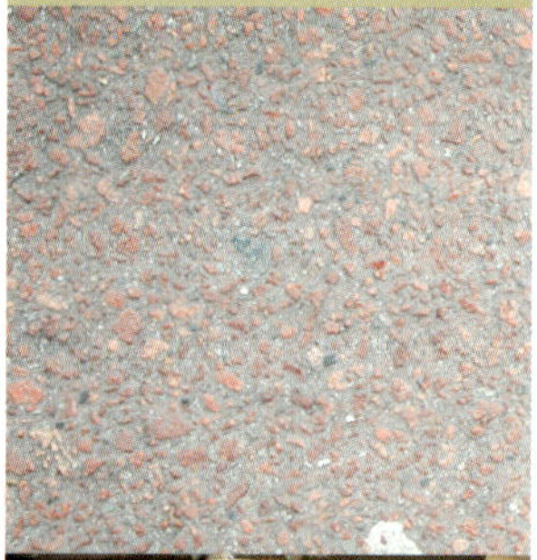
bicycle-path red

rust orange

architecture green

tree-bark green

water green

phonebox green

sky blue

DIXI portable-toilet blue

container blue

lamppost blue

wood grey

paving-stone grey

wood grey

Kliko compost-bin grey

car-paint white
road-marking yellow
postbox red
rubbish-bin green
paper-bag blue
asphalt black

road-marking white
Dutch Railways yellow
car-paint red
container green
speed-radar blue
ditch-water black

tailboard grey
number-plate yellow
rear-reflector red
Connexxion green
ANWB touring-club blue
night black

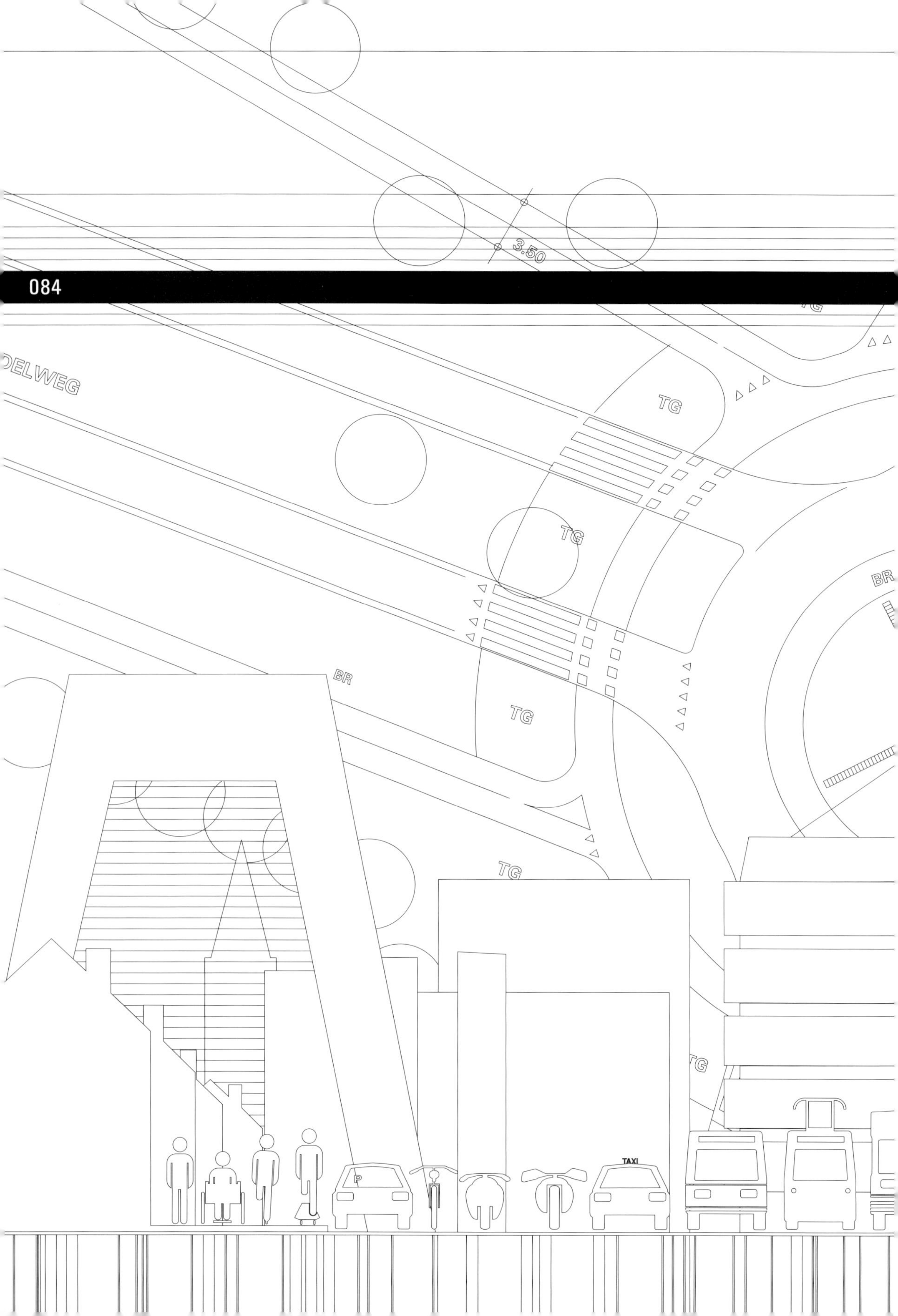
3.50
DELWEG
TG
TG
TG
TG
TG
TG
BR
BR
P
TAXI

SENSE OF MOVEMENT

The moving urban space

Arnold Reijndorp

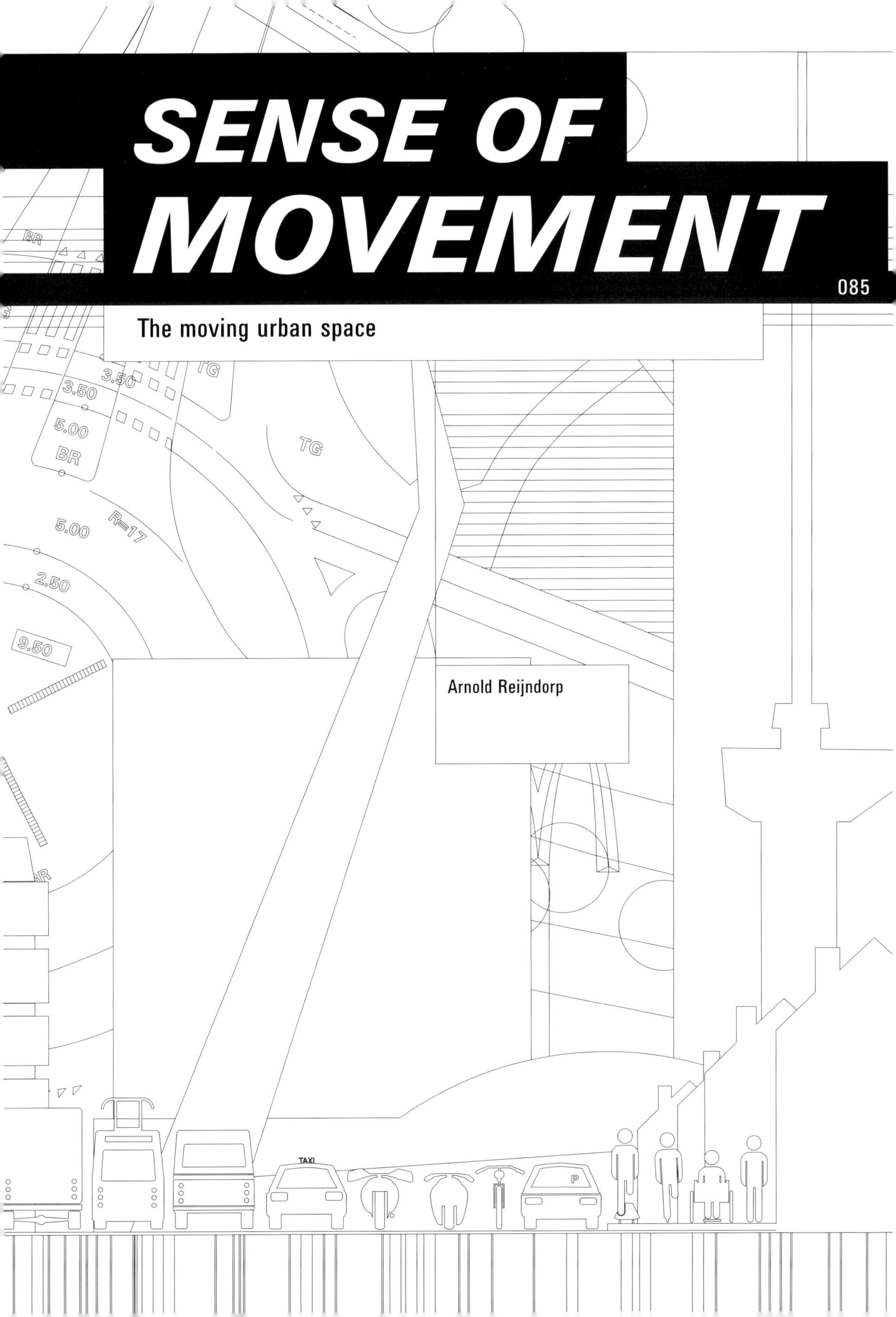

Every story is a travel story – a spatial practice.

(Michel de Certeau)

The 'Magazine' supplement to the weekend edition of *De Volkskrant* newspaper of January 4, 2003 included portraits of a selection of Dutch 'expats'. Besides the best restaurant, the most pleasant café and the most interesting attraction in the city where they now lived, they were also asked to name the most beautiful view.

The response of a young and successful art dealer who had left the Netherlands for New York was remarkable. He could have chosen for a dramatic answer by mentioning a view that since September 11, 2001 no longer exists, namely the view from the WTC. But instead of heading skyward for the most beautiful view, he headed underground: 'The most beautiful view is in the subway, where you see all the nationalities of the world.' And it is in this remarkable choice for that underground view that we hear the echo of the shock of September 11, because he continued: 'The wonder is that everyone feels they are a New Yorker and an American.' The sense of the city as an entity, as the 'concept city', expressed in painting in the cityscape and later in the photo of the 'skyline' or the view from a tall building, is linked here with the manifestation of the inhabitants of the city. The dynamism and pride of New York is no longer symbolized by the tall buildings, but by the diversity and energy of its population.

That population does not manifest itself as a totality, in a demonstration of harmony or metropolitan solidarity. The population that offers the most beautiful view of New York moves at high speed, in constantly changing configurations that depend on their motivating rationale, to a whole diversity of destinations. Their clothing, appearance and way of doing things reveals that many of them have come from far-off places in order to seek their fortune in this city. They do not talk with each other, hardly even look at each other, and they still seem somehow familiar with one another. 'Everyone feels like a New Yorker and an American!' And the place where you sense this most intensely is obviously that remarkable subterranean transport system which interconnects every part of that immense city and all its different groups of inhabitants. Even tourists pick up that feeling as soon as they have grasped some sense of how the system works. And then, for a couple of days, they also feel like a New Yorker, like a Parisian, Londoner or Berliner – they feel that they are part of a metropolis. It is this feeling, which seems to be evoked by the underground transport system, which, by analogy with a 'sense of place', you might call a 'sense of movement'.

Magic

'Sense of place' is an almost metaphysical notion, which some consider pure nonsense and others concede might well exist, but it certainly cannot be engineered or designed. Aldo Rossi implied that a 'magical' structure lies hidden beneath the surface of the city's architecture, which gives a place to daily life and specific events in a natural way. Pierre Bourdieu has pointed out that every instance of 'magic' is the result of the constant production of meanings by all kinds of people and institutions.

The specific 'feeling' evoked by a place emerges because of years of use by particular groups and because of ingrained routines, by which a place or route gains a particular atmosphere, reputation or 'name' – something which, over the course of time, can prove highly resilient. The fact that the structure of the physical space, in spite of the increasing importance of the virtual space of flows of information, has proven to be much more resilient than expected is therefore not only to the credit of past investments in the physical infrastructure but also the result of social and cultural factors.

The apparent shift in emphasis over recent years to 'flows' (the 'space of flows') would seem to make it necessary to replace the static notion of 'sense of place' by the much more dynamic-sounding sense of movement. However, this would show a lack of appreciation for the complex way in which movement and place jointly define space.

First of all, this increased mobility of people and information brings to life a whole range of new places. The network city is much more than a number of junctions at the intersection of different flows. Rather it is the evolution of a highly differentiated urban field, composed of 'red' and 'green', cultural and natural, rushed and peaceful, commercial and idealized places. The mobile citizen composes a personal space from these places. Movement is essential to the experience of space.

That is the second point, and it is nothing new. Let us return to the most beautiful view of New York. Michel de Certeau wrote his book *The Practice of Everyday Life* in an age when the WTC was still the proud symbol of New York. The chapter about 'spatial practices' starts with a view from the WTC, and de Certeau contrasts that distanced gaze with the experience of the city at street level: the voyeur in contrast with the participant. He quotes the text of a poster: 'It's hard to be down when you're up.' He actually arrives at the same conclusion as the Dutch art dealer cited above. The city as concept, the planned city, the city as an entity, is making a comeback. The city of quotidian activities, of pluriformity, is making a comeback. There is still a big gap between the perspective from above and the perspective from the street.

Choreography

Space, de Certeau states, is practised place. This is a rather difficult formulation for a distinction that other urban sociologists have made: they consider the built environment as a 'potential' environment, which can only be transformed into a social or cultural environment through use and by acquiring a history. In talking about 'spatial practices', de Certeau is primarily referring to movement: '... the street geometrically defined by urban planning is transformed into a space by walkers.'

The users of the city create social and cultural spaces by moving from one place to another. The difference between the 'space from above' and the 'space of movement' is encapsulated in the difference between maps and route directions. There are different ways to tell people the way. The first describes, as it were, a map: the theatre stands opposite the concert hall on the square at the end of this street. The second describes a route: at the next traffic lights you turn right, then continue straight on for a while, turn left at the church and then you are at the museum. Most people use this second kind of description. And although the maps as we know them have ultimately arisen from countless descriptions of routes by travellers, pilgrims and explorers, we are currently experiencing the reversal of that development: the road map is being replaced by the electronic voice of the car computer, which tells us where we must turn left or right. This once again ratifies de Certeau's argument that the city of the overview is being supplanted by the space of practice and routes. Whereas the map sets out the backdrop, the route description is choreography, a quick sketch of the movement between different points: a dance that continuously redefines the space.

Codes

The creation of that space as a collection of meaningful places and routes is less the result of set routines – for example between home and work – now than it once was. Mobility is a way to assemble a temporally variable 'city of choice'. The spaces of the urban field are characterized by criss-cross movements. Mapping this would produce the image of an inextricable ball of thread. This is because we are still accustomed to thinking in points and lines. But what de Certeau wrote about the street in 1984 also applies today to the connections in the network city. The users, the motorists, the commuters, the travellers and day-trippers transform the motorways, railways and their intersections into something much greater than traffic space.
The subway, as we have seen, is an example of this. Marc Augé is fascinated by the everyday routines that metro passengers perform, because it is for this very reason that the metro functions as a specific social space, with codes, rules and habits, which are the mark of every social space. This also applies to other traffic spaces: motorways, airports and stations. These spaces transform a highly diverse public into travellers. 'How can the Parisian possibly distinguish one metro station from the other?' Augé wonders.
'I see them go by every evening, at Sèvres-Babylone, squeezed like sardines in the subway cars or sprinting down the corridors – men and women, old and young, schoolchildren, secretaries, professors, employees, bums, Europeans, Africans, Gypsies, Asians, Americans – all these subterranean travelers so different from one another, whose almost regular movements (like those of the Atlantic Ocean, with its high and low tides and its periods of strong and dead waters) suggest nonetheless that they are animated, shaken, tossed together, and dispersed by the same force of attraction. Is the only thing these multiple solitudes have in common ... the not entirely fortuitous coincidence of their daily schedules?'
It is this sense of a remarkably diverse mass of people or vehicles, which with a single exception – and this immediately stands out as deviant – all fall in line with the unwritten rules, rituals and routines that determine the movement in and through that specific space, which characterizes the sense of movement. This does not turn the new traffic spaces into anonymous transit spaces, into the 'non-places' that Augé would later write about, but into specific social spaces that are then essentially no different to older urban spaces (streets, squares, boulevards), where the codes and rituals regulate the behaviour and use in the same way, though these might be different. This also distinguishes the practised users from the chance

passers-by. In the same way the commuter knows at exactly what point on the platform the doors of a metro carriage will open, the way in which some pedestrians negotiate their way through the jostling crowd or how taxi drivers exploit every available space in the stream of traffic betrays a high level of training.

Familiarity

Traffic spaces do not primarily derive their social and cultural significance from cultural events or social manifestations. Of course this is true of a few specific places, as it is no coincidence that routes of demonstrations coincide with those of centuries-old processions. An interesting shift is even observable here. Kristiaan Boret has pointed out a significant difference between demonstrations staged a few years ago about the kidnap and murder of a number of children in Belgium. One, a 'silent procession', proceeded on foot through the centre of Brussels and concluded with a demonstration at the city's Palace of Justice. The other, a memorial procession of thousands of motorcyclists, truckers and motorists, ended at the carpark of a giant department store on the periphery.
This shift from a monumental to a completely mundane setting demonstrates all the better that the defining forces in the symbolic economy of the space are not special events but everyday rituals and routines. The quotidian is marked by an odd combination of familiarity and surprise. What does familiarity mean today? Is it the street where you live, with the familiar neighbours and the shop on the corner where the shopkeeper greets you by name, or the landscape and the routines of the motorway that you use more or less frequently? An example from a favourite detective series of mine, in which the Italian commissioner Aurelio Zen is the chief character: 'Although Zen rarely drove if he could possibly help it, the neutral, extraterritorial domain of the *rete autostradale* never failed to have a similar calming effect on him. For the modest price of the toll, you were admitted to a private club that stretched the length and breadth of the country, a club that displayed an aristocratic disdain for regional traditions or quirks of topography, and was just about the only institution in the country guaranteed to be open twenty-four hours a day, every day of the year. Whether you were just outside Turin or 2,000 metres up in the Abruzzi mountains, the same rules applied and the same facilities were available.'
In his book *Fantasy City*, John Hannigan writes that fast-food chains like McDonalds are successful not just because they strive for a rationalization of production and distribution, but because they offer commonly understood signs and the same standardized procedures all over the world. The same is true for international hotel chains, airports, department stores and so on. Experiences from the past serve as a trusted guide, in a different city, in another part of the world. It is only when someone is seeking surprise, no matter how mundane, that one notices how familiar these routines are.
'As a regular patron of a downtown Burger King,' Hannigan writes, 'I have come to appreciate the concise, almost robotic four-question interrogation by the counter server: "What would you like? To drink? For here? Salt or ketchup?" Codes also apply for the local sandwich bar, but these are

specific. Not only can you choose from many more options than those listed, it is also unclear when it is your turn. This sometimes so confounds new customers that they often flee the premises. Everyone who has tried to order an espresso along with a piece of cake or a sandwich in an 'authentic' café in any Italian city has had the same experience. The espresso is manageable, but how do you get your hands on that little tart? Pointing does not work. First you have to get a little receipt from the matron standing behind the till opposite the bar. But what is that cake called in Italian?
We mourn the loss of local familiarity. This is logical, since it is part of our everyday routine, our way of life. Simultaneously we embrace the new global familiarity, which permits us to travel unencumbered and establishes a basis for the exploration of new surroundings. The local familiarity throws up a barrier for the outsider. Anyone who wants to taste the authentic 'sense of place' must first become familiar with the unwritten rules. And this is usually preceded by a journey through a familiar world where the rules and the language are the same everywhere. This creates a distinct travellers' language which is used at every airport. 'It is true that this language is based on English and increasingly on American, but it is replete with specific terms that are only understood by travellers, and which must be understood if travellers wish to avoid problems outside their home country.' (Mijksenaar)
The global space created in this way, which 'signifies' (literally providing signs as well as figuratively providing meanings), is not just a space for the rich and the powerful. That space, in which not only the business traveller but also the package tourist and the refugee know perfectly well how to find their way, is in fact democratized by the familiarity of the signs and the transparency of the routines. This new, everyday space is also increasingly becoming a space of protest, because protest no longer depends on the onlookers on the side of the street, but on the disturbance of everyday mobility and coverage in the media.

Myth

What is the relationship between those new, worldwide traffic spaces, in the sense intended by de Certeau, and the local public spaces of our 'scattered' cities? Sometimes they touch. More and more in fact, for example when the McDonalds on the motorway evolves into the ideal hangout for youths from the Rotterdam suburb of Hoogvliet. Or in the case of ring roads around cities which develop into a component of rapid, local routes.
Like some older urban spaces, the new traffic spaces seem able to acquire a mythical dimension and form the stage set for countless films and novels. What's more, it seems that many of those older spaces have lost their mythical power because of the disappearance of their traffic function. Is there anyone still able to connect the memories and images of the pre-war Potzdamerplatz, at that time the busiest and most modern traffic junction in Europe, with the environment that has been created there by Daimler Benz and Sony?
Since the 1980s, the increased consideration for the quality of public space has focused on the reinstatement of the 'repose and meeting function'. Traffic was primarily a necessary evil, designed according to functional

criteria, buried into the ground or hidden behind noise bafflers.
The sense of freedom, of broadening one's horizon and perspectives, of luxury and comfort, that had been associated with the sense of movement since the 1950s, has, as a concrete experience of the urban public space, vanished before our very eyes. Not that there has been any shortage of criticism about the negative effects of separating functions – in the evening and at night, car-free shopping centres looked desolate. However, this criticism failed to produce a re-evaluation of traffic as an element that gave meaning to the experience of the public space. Plans to permit motorized traffic at certain places in the inner city are also steadfastly rejected in Rotterdam. But for many people, a comparison of the Oude Hoogstraat (a pedestrian area) with the Meent (a classic shopping street) is likely to come out in favour of the latter.
On closer inspection, the distinction between stasis and movement does not appear to be the crux in the change in approach to the organization of space. It is much more important that the routes, which hitherto were the result of the activities of the users of the space, have become the object of spatial planning. Not residential areas but bus lanes and cycle routes formed the core of this turnaround in the 1980s, soon followed by recreational routes, the 'P-routes' leading to city carparks, and shopping circuits. The planners replaced the freedom of choice of the urban map, the potential environment that is their proper domain, with the regulation of spatial practices.
This has detracted from the significance and meaning of urban public space, in two ways. First of all, the stage on which the city's inhabitants used to perform their choreography has become fragmented and fenced off. Secondly, the myth of accessibility undermines the mythical potential of specific spaces, which is based on symbolism and ritual.

Theatre

What might an urbanism based on a sense of movement look like? It would involve consideration of possible routes and different worlds, but these are not the object of design; that is the urban map. This design makes possible the overlapping of different worlds. In some places this is strictly orchestrated. Where the combination of different types of traffic meets objections (because of the differences in speed, use of space or nuisance), the design organizes an overlap in the vertical plane, by stacking and interconnecting the maps tailored to the different speeds. OMA's plan for Almere's new city centre is the most concise example of this, but Rotterdam's 'spender's gulch' also falls into this category.
This new architecture of space harks back to the old distinction between the everyday (comedy), the monumental (tragedy) and the elusive (satire), but in a novel way. It acquiesces to the everyday annoyances and frustrations of gridlock and double parking, because these also constitute part of the congestion, without which the city as theatre would be unthinkable. But it also appreciates that some transitions demand a new form of monumentalism, as a resting point, turning point or connecting point where daily activity is briefly interrupted. That applies to special moments (weddings,

going out, jurisdiction), which demand a more symbolic arrangement of space (the opportunity to 'drive past', 'show off'), but also for the border crossings between global and local worlds. We see this in the 'renaissance' of the station building, whether in railways, the metro or the airport. Within that everyday world, with monumental elements here and there, the satire unfolds unhindered. These are, of course, the skaters and the scooters, but let us not forget that there are a growing number of people-movers and rolling sidewalks.

In the design of the traffic space, in a word, attention is shifting from 'accessibility' to 'symbolism'. With both its new bridge and its new metro line, Rotterdam has chosen to step up the theatrical aspect of mobility. The new bridge in particular, which draws automobile traffic right through the city, seems like sheer craziness from a traffic management perspective. But in terms of the city as theatre, the creation of a backdrop against which the city's users and visitors can perform their personal and yet collective choreographies, at different speeds and moving in different directions, this bridge is a sublime stage.

Bibliography

Marc Augé, *Un ethnologue dans le métro*, Paris, 1986. English translation: *In the Metro*, trans. Tom Conley, Minneapolis, 2002, p. 42

Marc Augé, *Non-Places. Introduction to an Anthropology of Supermodernity*, trans. John Howe, London, 1995

Kristiaan Borret, 'Over domeinen. Het publieke, het private en het collectieve/ 'On Domains. The Public, the Private and the Collective', in *Oase*, no. 54, winter 2001, pp. 50-61

Pierre Bourdieu, '*Vive la crise*! For Heterodoxy in Social Science', in *Theory and Society*, vol. 17, 1988, pp. 773-787

Michel de Certeau, *The Practice of Everyday Life*, trans. Steven F. Rendall, Berkeley/Los Angeles/London, 1984

Michael Dibdin, *And Then You Die. An Aurelio Zen Mystery*, London, 2002

Paul Mijksenaar, 'Nederlands weg op Schiphol? [4] Eens', in *Onze Taal*, vol. 71, 2002, p. 269

John Hannigan, *Fantasy City. Pleasure and Profit in the Postmodern Metropolis*, London/New York, 1998

Aldo Rossi, *The Architecture of the City*, trans. Diane Ghirardo and Joan Ockman, Cambridge, Mass., 1984

TRAFFIC INTERVENTIONS – THE EVERYDAY AND THE UNUSUAL

Traffic infrastructure is often designed to be unobtrusive, but that does not mean that lengthy study has not gone into it. Interventions are intended to improve existing situations, increase safety or lead to a better enforcement of the rules. Designing interventions in such a way that everyone instinctively understands and applies them is quite an art.

Dolf Broekhuizen

Driving lanes on Dutch roadways have been separated by white lines since the 1920s. Initially, only wide roads and curves were lined; nowadays there is not a single stretch of asphalt without white, yellow or blue stripes. One exception few road users will have noticed is the Erasmus Bridge: the on and off ramps are marked, but there is no marking on the bridge itself, because of an efficient traffic flow. The carriageway on the bridge is narrower than two separate driving lanes yet wide enough to allow two cars to drive side by side. When it is quiet, cars drive in single file at relatively high speed to the exit lanes at the traffic lights. When traffic is busier, motorists drive more slowly – this allows them to drive side by side, and they form two lanes before they reach the traffic lights.

Erasmus Bridge carriageway

There are unusual zebra crossings in various places in Rotterdam's shopping centre, such as at the intersection of the busy Aert van Nesstraat and the Lijnbaan pedestrian area. At this spot, the zebra stripes have been extended across the entire breadth of the Lijnbaan. Because the dark paving of the shopping street has also been continued, a broad speed bump has been created. The large size, the different colour, the material used and the speed bump are all signals to the motorist to be alert. Without turning it into a pedestrian crossing with traffic lights, which would have interrupted the pedestrian area of the Lijnbaan, a protected and comfortable crossing has been devised.

Lijnbaan – Aert van Nesstraat zebra crossing

Before this bridge was built, cyclists coming from the Schouwburgplein or the Aert van Nesstraat alongside the Pauluskerk had to turn right, into the one-way traffic on the Mauritsweg. The new bridge (2002) provides a quick bicycle connection between the shopping and entertainment heart of the city and the west. In addition, the bridge makes it easier to reach the footpath and sculpture trail along the singel, or canal promenade. However, there was no space and no money to build a 'standard' bicycle bridge; moreover, such a bridge would have spoiled the intended spatial design. An unconventional solution was found: the bicycle bridge was designed as a pedestrian bridge. The lowered kerb is the sole indicator that cyclists are tolerated here – thanks to the design, the cyclists defer to the pedestrians. So far this idea is working so well that not all cyclists have caught on that they are allowed to use the bridge. The bicycle bridge over the Westersingel awaits further discovery.

096

Westersingel bicycle bridge

To increase traffic safety for cyclists at intersections with automobile traffic, the letters 'OFOS' have been painted on the carriageway at traffic lights – this stands for 'Opgeblazen Fiets Opstel Strook' ('Expanded Cycle Lane'). The principle is simple and extremely effective: the stop line for cars has been moved back, and cyclists may use the entire breadth of the carriageway, in front of the cars, to wait at the traffic light. This gives them a head start on the cars. When traffic moves forward on green, motorists have a far better view of the cyclists. Traffic safety is served in two ways. Cyclists going straight ahead are less likely to be struck by cars wanting to turn right, and cyclists who without OFOS had hardly any chance to turn left, because of the cars coming up behind them, can now cross the intersection first.

Aert van Nesstraat 'OFOS' cycle lane

On the Coolsingel, parked bicycles are used as a barrier between the shopping public and the automobile traffic. Multiple rows of stainless steel bicycle stands have been placed between the bicycle path and the carriageway. Outside shop business hours, when there are no bicycles, the stands form a line of unobtrusive arches. During business hours, however, parked bicycles swell these arches into a dense hedge that protects the users of the bicycle path and the pedestrian boulevard from the automobile traffic and the trams. In addition, the hedge of bicycles encourages pedestrians to use the zebra crossings to cross the Coolsingel.

Coolsingel bicycle stands

Familiar elements of any Dutch city centre are the speed bumps, raised kerbs, bollards and lift-barriers to divide, divert, slow or direct traffic. The variety of solutions is overwhelming: bollards that sink into the ground by remote control, posts that can be removed with a key, three-sided traffic cones that can be collapsed, lift-barriers with magnetic cards, chains across the street surface, reflective bumps to prevent lorries parking on top of a metro tunnel, artificial stone spheres or metal bollards to keep cars off historic streets and finally concrete troughs that can only be traversed by buses and rubbish-collection vehicles. Not using such physical barriers means hoping for good driving behaviour, a hope often disappointed.

Car-free zone bollards

In 2000, a skate park appeared in the central reservation of the Blaak thoroughfare. Ever since, skaters in the midst of the through traffic have been a point of animation in the busy life of the city. To strengthen the identity of the skate park in this isolated location, its asphalt has been painted with red and blue areas, to a design by graphic designers J. de Vries and J. Bekkers. The points where other traffic intersects the skate park have also been painted. Because standard white lines have been used, the marking meets all traffic-engineering requirements. The space in between, however, has been painted in divergent colours and patterns. Cars pass over red asphalt, cyclists follow paths of diagonal blue stripes, and there are red-and-white lanes for pedestrians. The effect is that skaters realize that they are on the edge of a dangerous area, while other road users are given a signal to watch out for the skaters.

Blaak skate park

The Rotterdam city centre includes a large pedestrian area, where great hordes of people come to shop or otherwise spend their leisure time. Every so often a tinkling tram makes its appearance in the midst of the crowd of shoppers. The encounter between tram and pedestrian defies the usual practice of segregating dissimilar traffic flows with viaducts, barriers or tunnels. None of that on the Lijnbaan: the tram rails are simply countersunk in the surface of the pedestrian area, marked off only by stainless steel dots. Pedestrians are alerted to an approaching tram by warning signs and sound and light signals; the tram also adjusts its speed. The unavoidable confrontation between the demands of an unobstructed tramline and an uninterrupted, car-free shopping street forms a new balance here.

Lijnbaan tram crossing

On the east side of the Kralingse Plas lake runs a long straight path designed in the 1990s within the scope of the restructuring of this city park. The route has been shifted: a slight dip at either end leads strollers to the path along the water's edge. The dip makes this route unappealing to cyclists. The path is several hundred metres long, covered with fine gravel and flanked by a row of benches. This configuration is an invitation to stroll, to stop and contemplate, and makes it unusable for skaters. These interventions make the boulevard exclusive to the pedestrian and introduce a new element in the 'Hollandse Boslandschap' ('Holland Woods Landscape') of the 1930s. In the original configuration of the park, the paths provided a view of nature through the clumps of trees. From the path along the water there is now a view of the Rotterdam skyline behind the clumps of trees. Through this intervention the focus is no longer so much on an experience of nature as on an experience of nature within the city.

Kralingse Plas footpath

In the southwest corner of Rotterdam, industrial sites and docklands are situated next to nature and recreation areas. Road traffic to the industrial areas in the Botlek, Europoort and the Maasvlakte is kept strictly separate from the recreational users around the Brielse Meer and Oostvoornse Meer lakes. Within the docklands, cyclists are not allowed anywhere on the carriageway, but they can use recreational routes. The long distances and the empty area are invitations to speed – this results in hazardous conditions for both automobile and slower traffic. Traffic safety has been increased by applying an unusual marking system: instead of a line down the middle of the road, stripes have been painted one metre in from either side. This makes cars drive down the middle of the carriageway and give cyclists more room. When cars approach one another from opposite directions, they not only move to the side, but this marking system also makes them reduce speed.

Docklands recreational route

THE TEMPO OF THE CITY

Florian Boer

Relative time

The city is on the move. People commute from home to office, from the office to the lunch café, from the café to a friend's house, from the girlfriend's place to the gym, from the club to the lounge, to the park, back home, to the supermarket, to the shops, to the petrol station, to.... Besides being these many destinations, the city is primarily a place where you are on the move. Travel is a daily activity that to a large extent also determines our experience of our surroundings. The time we spend doing this is more important than the distance covered. Time is the measure by which we compose the 'mental map' of the city. This perception of time is so important, in fact, that there seems to be a 'law of preservation of travel time': around the world, people spend an average of 1.1 hours travelling per day. This applies to developing countries as well as to the Western world. As soon as people are able to travel faster, this seems to be translated into their covering greater distances. The time expended is a constant factor, an equilibrium sought time and again.

Time, however, is relative: to a large extent, what you experience determines 'how long you experience it'. The 'tempo' is defined as a personal experience of the time expended. The 'tempo of the city' starts with the subjective perception of travel time and the travel choices that can be made on this basis. This mobile use of the city is directly connected to the way in which the traffic system is organized. In turn, the current system and the plans relating to it influence the way in which the city will be used in the future. To a certain degree this is at odds with the spatial and programmatic cohesion of the city as it currently stands, and thus also with its urban planning. The central issue for which we are trying to make some connections is how urban planning might be better equipped to deal with the tempo of the city. In this essay we use the city of Rotterdam as our model, approaching the central question from three different angles: perception of travel time, organization of the transport system and impact on spatial organization.

Travel planner

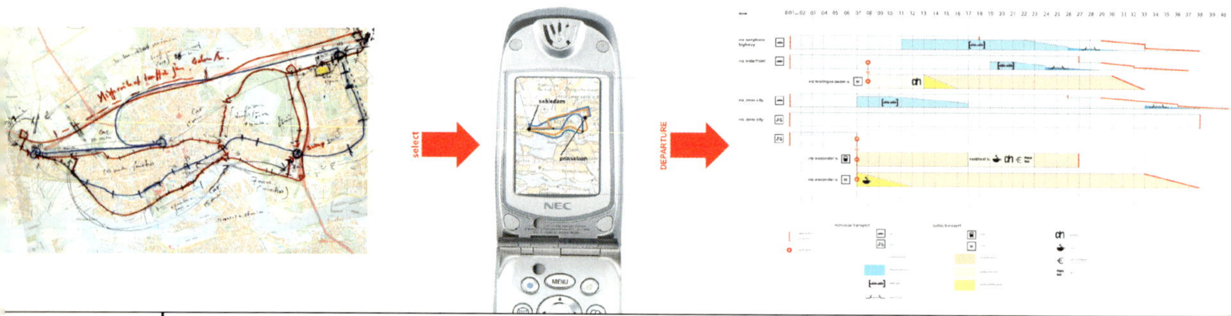

Study of the travel options through Rotterdam based on two randomly selected points. See the explanation in the box on page 108.

Travelling is a question of briefly residing somewhere, not only because you can experience and participate in things while moving but also because you can also actually do things. The electronic devices that have become part and parcel of urban transport make parallel experiences possible. The mobile phone, the MP3 player and the laptop are all devices which allow you to create your own surroundings at any given place – not in the literal sense of making something physically or spatially, but mentally. With your favourite tape resounding through your head you can imagine that you are somewhere other than the street you are cycling through at that moment. In the car there is a growing range of devices that help the motorist or passengers to do myriad things simultaneously, so that the fact that you are on the road has actually become a side issue. However, the fact that driving has come to be of secondary importance is dangerous too, and has led to recent legislation to enforce 'hands-free' calling. The motorist can lead his or her own life, as if in a kind of self-sufficient capsule, independent of the place where the motorist actually is. The choices have increased enormously. A mode of transport does not merely ferry you from A to B: 'Travel time is activity time!' This means that moving through the urban space is perceived differently to just moving. The journey is designed on the basis of the desired use of time in combination with the possibilities offered by the chosen mode of transport.

Travelling by bike demands more mobile and more compact devices than does the car. The level of comfort influences behaviour: on a tram you are less likely to open your laptop than on a train. The way in which the traffic lights are harmonized with each other and wave the motorist smoothly through green across the city, for instance, are also contributing factors. Being able to spend one's travel time usefully is connected to the reliability. If you know that the journey takes half an hour, with as minimal a risk of unexpected delays as possible, then the journey can be tailored to this. Unexpected setbacks in the journey time constitute a significant emotional delay. A longer than anticipated journey is less terrible when you have been able to take that into account. It is psychologically shortened if you can spend this time usefully with some activity or other, even if just for relaxation, but the mode of transport must offer you a certain level of comfort. The duration of the journey itself is also a defining factor in this: different means are employed for ten minutes than for a whole hour.

At the end of a hard day's work you might want to take a quiet route, from where you can watch a beautiful sunset, or contemplate the unfolding panorama of city lights being illuminated while you are waiting at the traffic lights. If your surroundings contribute to your journey, the time is perceived as relatively short and the journey feels less like 'lost' time. Besides the spatial pleasure, there can also be programmatic enjoyment offered on or alongside the transport network: the road that passes a pleasant bar where you meet friends, or the station where you can have a cup of coffee or do other on-the-hoof shopping before departure, on arrival or while transferring. The ability to choose among various travel options to reach a particular destination is, after all, a decidedly 'metropolitan pleasure'. The frequency of public transport, transfer facilities, the finely meshed networks of public transport, car and bike – all these factors contribute to a multifaceted 'city experience'.

Perceived travel time is determined by four factors: speed, reliability, comfort and pleasure. Alongside the possibilities in the interior of the chosen means of transport, it is the traffic system that plays a key role here. A study into a journey within Rotterdam's urban/metropolitan network (see sidebar) compared a variety of possible routes which are theoretically not so dissimilar in actual duration, but are certainly different in terms of the degree of reliability, comfort and pleasure. The traffic system turned out to be 'multimodal' for this sample route: it offers choices in transport modes and also offers the possibility of switching from one mode to another along the way. Each route offers a different way of moving through the city, and therefore a different perceptual perspective on and experience of the city.

Travelplanner

An example for a cursory study into different ways of travelling is the journey from a house in the Alexander Polder to Schiedam-Centrum railway and metro station. Following the opening of the east-west metro extension, seven more or less comparable options seem to be available. These include various motorways and various possible intermodal transfer hubs.

The motorway is theoretically the quickest, but only if there are no traffic jams. The reliability of the A20 around here is not high, but this could be improved with up-to-date information. By using Dynamic Traffic Management Systems (DTMS), the city council is striving to inform motorists of current conditions at various places in the city using electronic information boards. These are placed at strategic decision-making points in the transport network, so that you can change course if the route planned is suddenly obstructed by delays. This strategy will once again make the high-speed routes reliable.

The bicycle is without doubt the most reliable mode of transport, and it is not even the slowest. This is partly thanks to the fact that the cyclist moves relatively independently of the waiting times at traffic lights. The distance from door to door actually involves a simple calculation using geographical distance and average cycling speed. What's more, cyclists get the most pleasure from fine weather and undoubtedly enjoy the best view.

The train offers the best chance of a rapid connection, with a transfer at the Central Station. If the NS (Dutch Railways) does its job properly then this journey is also highly pleasurable: you have enough time to buy a newspaper and drink a cappuccino during the transfer.

The most attractive option is the motorway that meanders along with the river via the Maas Boulevard and offers beautiful and varying panoramas of the cityscape. As with all the motorways through or around 'the centre', this one is most unreliable at rush hour. Transferring to the metro at Kralingse Zoom presents a quicker alternative. The further you live from the Alexander metro station, the more sensible a short car ride to the Kralingse Zoom. The short waiting times on the metro and the ease of parking balance out against the bridging of the geographically shorter distance to the closest metro station, where the metro also rides less frequently.

An isochronous city

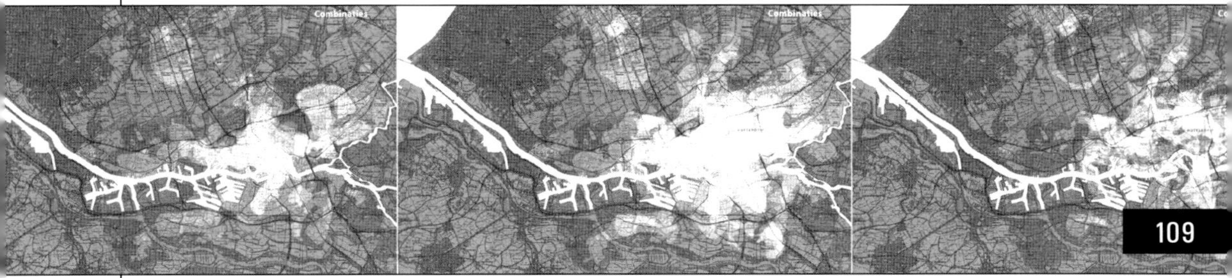

Accessibility by public transport within 30 minutes from seven Rotterdam nodes

1. The situation in 1998, the benchmark year
2. The target scenario in 2020
3. The increase in accessibility in 2020 compared with 1998

Behind the temporal perception of infrastructure lies a world of traffic models. The entire Rotterdam region has been assimilated in a mathematical model of traffic movements classified by point of departure, destination and the effect on all the traffic spaces in between. From a chosen point in the city it is possible to calculate to the minute how long it will take to travel to all the other points in the Rotterdam region included in the model. The results of all these time calculations are compiled into an 'isochronous' representation of the city. This is like a time zone projected onto the geographical map of the city and represents how long it takes to travel from a specific point to surrounding areas with the mode of transport chosen.
In the traffic model used by the city authorities the calculation always starts from a single point. By combining multiple points, each time taking the shortest travel time, this delineates an 'accessibility profile' for Rotterdam.
It is interesting that the *Ruimtelijk Plan Rotterdam* ('Spatial Plan for Rotterdam', the city's urban policy through 2010) is based on seven future modes, around which the accessibility must be organized.[1] This takes into account not only the city's current polycentric functioning but also projects this into the future. The city council's ambition is to make the entire Rotterdam region accessible within 45 minutes by public transport, from at least one of the seven specified nodes in the city. The effect of this is best seen in the projected public transport lines, intended to connect the various nodes without the need to travel via Rotterdam's Central Station. In fact public transport will then be able to do what the car already does: describe a less hierarchical network. Perhaps the 'Central Station' should be renamed at that point.
The isochronous maps are a representation of the network city: the city that is shaped by flows, connections and nodes instead of by formal, hierarchical or spatial structures. Now that the functional and formal structures coincide less and less frequently, the question is whether the legibility of the dynamic city still has anything to do with spatial cohesion. Time orders the use of the network city, which is based on the possibilities presented by the infra-structure network. Does the 'tempo of the city' form a different basis for its spatial planning? An initial answer is that the city may indeed be legible, but

the continuity does not necessarily coincide with the formal structure of the city. The functional infrastructure is continuous, but the programmatic and spatial continuity are highly variable and are even absent in many places. This stands in sharp contrast with the 19th-century enclosed cityscape, which still forms the city's frame of reference for many. In this city, the structures that organized it spatially, made it functionally accessible and were programmatically significant worked as one. A familiar example of this is the system of boulevards in Paris, which formed the basis for the spatial planning of the entire city. In the modern city, these three functions are usually no longer united.

Nowadays, for example, the metro plays an important role in the experience of the fragmented city as an entity. The Rotterdam's metro map gives an excellent impression of the organization of Rotterdam, in which all the centres are carefully interconnected by two neat lines: a red one and a blue one. The bigger the city, the more important this system is for the use of the city. Many metropolises can only be understood from their metro systems and the logic that these systems offer. The time factor related to this orders the city, and the way the city is understood. Sometimes it is still possible to find the rudiments of a formal structure being used functionally, but this is usually on a smaller, more local scale. On the larger scale, one has to search hard to find other ways of representing the city.

The tempographic city

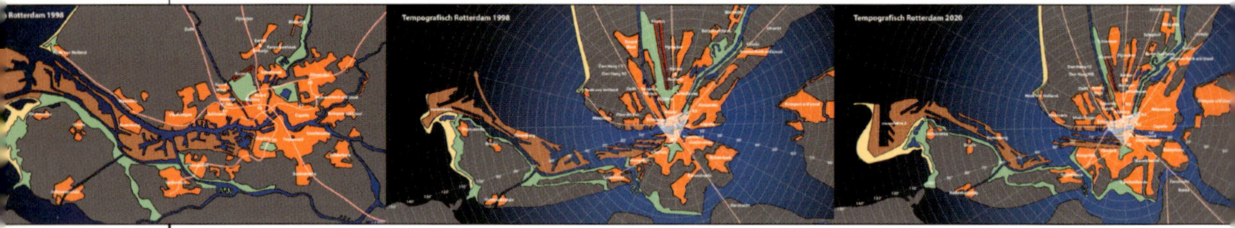

A tempographic representation of accessibility by public transport in Rotterdam, based on seven nodes

1. Geographical rotterdam 1998
2. Tempographic Rotterdam 1998
3. Tempographic Rotterdam 2020

Imagine that the city exists not as it is represented geographically, but as a function of the amount of time it takes to get through it, to it or away from it. Such a map, based on a timescale instead of a geographic scale, is called a tempographic representation. In contrast with an isochronous map, where geographical distances are measurable while time is represented without a scale, the tempographic map displays a measurable timeline and geography without a scale. Because the traffic models calculate distances from a single point, durations have to be calculated for many 'timed' distances, and these are collated in order to allow a depiction of the city in a meaningful form.

Direct representation would produce an illegible result and requires drastic simplification of the geographical data, as well as choices about what will be shown on the map.
The form of transport to be represented is the most basic choice. Public transport and the car produce very different maps. The Rotterdam *Ruit* (literally the 'Diamond', the rhomboid system of urban motorways) is very familiar and could almost be read as a logo. The Ruit organizes the city's accessibility by car on the basis of its exits, which is demonstrated by the burgeoning programme so close to these motorway entry and exit ramps. Public transport is primarily oriented around the seven nodes mentioned above. Because most changes will take place in this respect in the near future, it was decided to map out a representation of the public transport. The tempographic map can then also be compared directly with the isochronous map.
Between the stations of Schiedam, Alexander and Zuidplein, the whole urban territory has been shrunk into a compact 'urban triangle'. Within this everything is 'flattened', as it were, in terms of accessibility. This urban triangle is actually the modern public-transport network version of the historic port triangle on the Maas. The subtleties of the network within this urban area are set aside in favour of a tempographic representation of the whole Rotterdam region. In this imploded world, stations that lie far away seem to be next door, while some areas that are geographically 'next door' seem inaccessible. In future, from the 'central area' between the seven nodes, we will be able to travel just as quickly to Schiphol Airport as to Breda, Spijkenisse, The Hague or the Hook of Holland. Recreational areas, by contrast, seem to be poorly accessible by public transport, while public transport could present an ideal alternative to the great automobile migration that gears up in tandem with fine weather.
The tempographic model of the city primarily tells us about its usage patterns. The map shows a city that presents itself in its links to other urban places. Someone from Rotterdam can shop just as easily in other urban locations, in the same way other urbanites visit Rotterdam's shops. The cultural significance of this extends far beyond a more quickly accessible environment – it is instead a question of choosing one's personal city from the variety of urban places on offer in combination with the different forms of transport available. Channel-hopping behaviour is not limited to the dozens of TV channels available these days; it continues when you leave the house and go out into the streets. Everyone puts together his or her own city based on the mode of mobility selected. The tempo of the city is a personal film, and just like in the cinema, it is interwoven with 'flashbacks' and 'subplots'. The thread running through it is formed by the physical infrastructure that offers the best combination of speed, reliability, comfort and pleasure.
This fact has an impact on the spatial planning of the city. For the car this impact is probably even greater than it is for public transport systems, because the road network is more directly confronted with the formal structure of the city. That structure is usually no longer tailored to more intensive use of the car. Rapid routes follow the path of least resistance, no matter what the spatial logic. All that is required of the road system is that signposting be clear. Alternatives must be easily legible in case another route needs to be selected. A certain dynamic logic is of course important, as

backtracking is never a good way of making progress, and the networks should also be finely intermeshed. 'Routing' is increasingly performed by GPS devices, alongside which new user options for the capsule are evolving at a rapid pace. The result is that the motorist is increasingly becoming a passenger in his or her own car. A less hierarchical and more flexible network facilitates ease of use. Just as in the strategy adopted for public transport, there is no longer just a single centre operating like a trap for all the traffic.

Future urban planning will focus increasingly on maximizing the options offered by the traffic system; more geared to the planning and use of infrastructures. In this context, urban planning and traffic control are interrelated disciplines that provide the choreography for the city's circulatory dance. That requires a different attitude towards movement that is alert to opportunities for optimizing usage and for broadening the infrastructure's public significance.

Programmatic flexibility is a key to multiple spatial usage. Instead of physically stacking or extending, the physical structure can encompass different usage at different times without taking up any more space. Such a design would entail the organization of a time schedule for the existing infrastructure: a kind of choreographed flow. That in turn would require the layout of the road profile to be rethought: for instance, changing the direction of the traffic-flow during the morning and evening rush-hours (suggesting that tramlines should no longer be placed in the centre of the road). Traffic flows can be influenced by increasing or decreasing traffic-calming devices.

The traffic system can also acquire a multiple significance by injecting the infrastructure with the quality of social space. Parking solutions, for example, could serve as more than just garage spaces, they could also be urban destinations, places where people meet and relax, or just simply a spot with a stunning view. Rotterdam still lacks a real multi-storey car park in which the combined presence of hundreds of motorists would provide an unprecedented vertical light-show.

Of course, developments of this nature are applicable to both traditional city centres and the more peripheral areas that have long since attained the status of urban locations.

The data used was gathered by the 'Knowledge Centre', Traffic and Transport division, the Department for Urban Planning, Housing and Traffic (dS+V), City of Rotterdam. My special thanks to Harko Stolte for his feedback and suggestions. This essay is based on the study 'TM.RPT.2001' carried out by –scape for the Traffic and Transport division, Department for Urban Planning, Housing and Traffic (dS+V) of the City of Rotterdam. Contributors to the research by –scape were Pier Helder, Diego Barajas, and Florian Boer, in association with Jan Jongert. Thanks are also due to employees of the City of Rotterdam – Harko Stolte, Wilco Verhagen and Leo de Jonge – for their invaluable input.

1. The seven Public Transport nodes cited in the Rotterdam policy are: Alexander, Kralingse Zoom, Parkstad (near the Kuip stadium), Zuidplein, Schieveste (Schiedam centre), Noordrand and Central Station.

DARK SIDES

Mobility is crucial to contemporary society, but it has many dark sides.

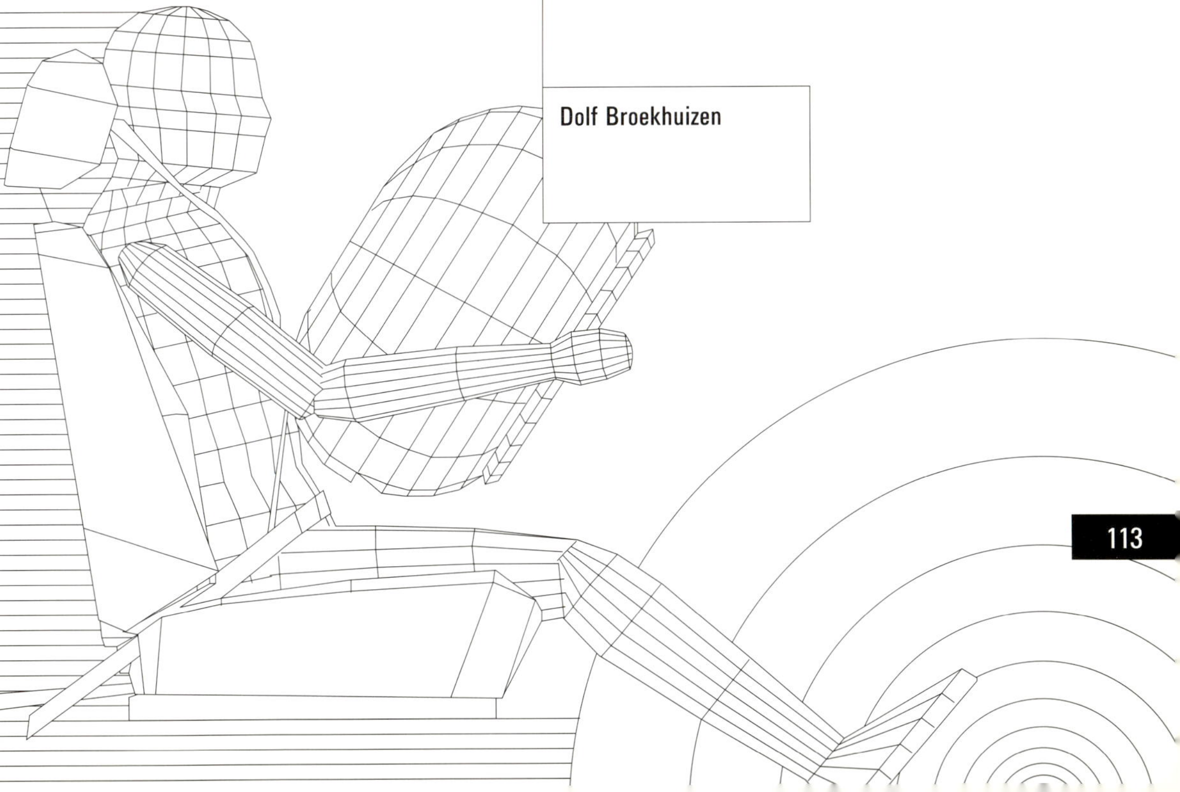

Dolf Broekhuizen

The air quality in the Rhine Delta area is poor in comparison with many other areas of the Netherlands. This is mainly due to industry, but the busy traffic in the region also plays a part. The last ten years have seen an improvement, thanks to the use of cleaner fuel and cleaner engines in new cars. In a period in which traffic increased by 16 percent, carbon dioxide emissions may have increased by about the same percentage, but on the other hand, pollution due to carbon monoxide, nitrogen oxides, sulphur dioxide, particulates and volatile organic materials has been reduced by 33 to 50 percent. Almost no lead compounds are being emitted any longer. Traffic in the Rhine Delta still releases 4.5 kilos of lead into the air, and 403 tonnes of particulates. Confirmation that emissions are not getting worse comes from the number of butterfly species that are considered indicators of the natural quality of a given area. Counts show that the populations of indicator species remain stable. Official butterfly areas, more and more of which are appearing along roads and paths, in Hoogvliet and in the Kralingse Bos woodlands, for example, are to be taken as optimistic testimony.

Mobility refuse

Intensive traffic creates a huge mountain of refuse. Every year hundreds of thousands of cars are discarded and millions of tyres wear out. Bicycles end up in the canals or are abandoned at the stations. Even maintenance on roads, such as relaying asphalt or replacing pavement tiles, creates refuse. Over the years, waste disposal has improved and reuse has become widespread. It would be even better for the environment not to create refuse in the first place. Measures aimed at reducing traffic, such as the promotion of carpooling, the building of transferia, experiments with light rail and the introduction of toll zones, fit into this.

The degradation of the public space can be clearly gauged by litter on the street. Fewer and fewer people feel responsible for what happens on the street, and so litter piles up and rubbish is put out on random days. But it is equally hard to believe what gets tossed out of moving cars or in parking lots. New methods of rubbish collection are needed, for example containers on the street accessible day and night. A more fanciful invention to combat litter is the *blikvanger* (in Dutch, a pun meaning both 'eye-catcher' and 'can-catcher') alongside roads and bicycle paths. These rubbish receptacles for aluminium cans take the form of conical nets and are placed, for example, alongside routes used by large numbers of school children. At the traffic lights at the end of some exits off motorways, the catchy 'blikvanger' may have to pay the price of its own success. It distracts motorists too much and thus creates a traffic hazard.

boundaries of social and ecological zones, dividing lines between rich and poor, or between nature and city. On motorways such as Rotterdam's 'Ruit' (the rhomboid-like 'Diamond' of motorways around the city) regulation on non-built-up areas has reinforced the corridor effect. All manner of intervention is being used to try to soften the negative impact of these boundaries. Between Prinsenland and the Kralingse Bos woodlands, bicycle and pedestrian tunnels have been dug under the Ruit. In the Ruigeplaatbos woodland on the edge of Hoogvliet, an attempt is being made to let the greenbelt structure form an uninterrupted ribbon. Yet these remain stopgap measures. As traffic intensifies, the barriers multiply and exert greater impact.

Space claims for parking areas

Residential areas are becoming ever more clogged up because of the increase in mobility. Whereas the number of housing units in an area remains constant and the number of residents is falling, car ownership by household has risen over the years. Parking is the main problem. A car is in use only five percent of the time; the rest of the time it stands still. Rotterdam, a city of 160,000 cars, needs an area the size of 200 football pitches to park all those cars. In the old residential neighbourhoods, what this leads to can clearly be seen: the once sizable and green public space has become a sea of metal. The environmental quality of districts such as Blijdorp and Pendrecht suffers. In new construction of large buildings in the city, inclusion of parking facilities within the building is increasingly required. In new residential developments the car is accorded more space, and alternatives are sought to parking on the street, in parking cellars, for example, under decks or on top of housing.

Social safety

Permanent security cameras are a sensitive issue in the debate about social safety on the street. In tunnels and on public transport, however, closed-circuit video surveillance in connection with traffic safety is highly valued. Since the pedestrian and bicycle path in the Maas Tunnel has been monitored by security cameras, the unsafe situations that predominated here have disappeared. The Rotterdam metro (RET) even puts out advertisements in which security cameras are highlighted as a positive selling point. Security cameras in the stations, manned from a central command centre, in combination with surveillance patrols and intensive cooperation with the police, is supposed to increase safety in the stations and on the metro.

The construction of infrastructure leaves behind residual areas in the city: scraps of wasteland where hardly anything happens. In the 1930s attempts were made to put the inner area of traffic intersections to use as parking for snowploughs, ambulances and road service vehicles. Small businesses opened premises under the arches of railway viaducts. It proved hardly practicable, because of the noise, pollution, vibrations and – strangely enough – the inaccessibility of the locations. Architects continue to find residual areas and construction on and around the motorway a fascinating subject. They look for opportunities to combine architecture and infrastructure. In Rotterdam experimental plans have been drawn up for entire cities on, alongside and under the motorways. Although the visionary designs have not yet gone beyond the drawing-board stage, construction alongside infrastructure is on the increase, especially along the Ruit.

Automobile traffic is the greatest source of noise pollution in the Netherlands. In Rotterdam, the ring of motorways of the Ruit (literally the 'Diamond', the rhomboid pattern of four motorways ringing the city) causes the primary nuisance. The postwar housing blocks at the Kleinpolderplein and the hamlet of Oud-IJsselmonde near the Van Brienenoord Bridge demonstrate that motorways and residential areas actually cannot exist side by side. Policy to address the nuisance is primarily aimed at combating symptoms. This means noise barriers, covered or sunken roadways, noise-reducing asphalt (double-layer porous asphalt concrete, or 'ZOAB') and the installation of sound insulation and extra-thick glazing in houses. These measures are only partially effective. They reduce the nuisance to an acceptable level, but the nuisance of the traffic speeding by remains. Rotterdam now has about 90 kilometres of noise barriers, and yet there are hardly any areas in or around the city where the traffic is not audible.

Isolation

Social isolation is a societal problem that in some aspects overlaps with mobility. As cities are increasingly laid out around the motorways, citizens without cars are increasingly unable to reach certain facilities, or can reach them only with difficulty. Fear of the outside world also keeps people from being mobile and venturing into the public space. A change in the service schedule can be a reason for an elderly person to stay at home. The lack of accessible kerbs or not feeling safe is also immobilizing. One regularly hears people say, 'I don't dare ride my bike anymore', 'I always lock my door at night', 'I lock the car doors these days when I'm driving' and 'I don't dare go into the shopping centre alone anymore'.

Lack of traffic safety: accidents

In the last hundred years numerous measures have been implemented to increase traffic safety, and with success. Thanks to guardrails, safety belts, air bags, road salt, traffic lights and numerous technological inventions, the huge increase in traffic has been matched by a drop in the number of traffic casualties. Yet many accidents still occur. In Rotterdam, 25 people die in traffic accidents every year and 30,000 people are involved in a traffic accident, either as the person responsible or as the victim. In an expression of the great emotional impact of each individual fatality, monuments have recently been placed along roadways by the victims' loved ones, as silent witnesses to a deadly accident and a personal place of remembrance.
A standard memorial has also been devised (designed by 3VN, the Dutch traffic safety organization) entirely in accordance with the safety requirements set for public highways. This black silhouette of a standing figure is more a new sort of traffic sign urging road users to be careful than something offering loved ones an occasion for personal grief.

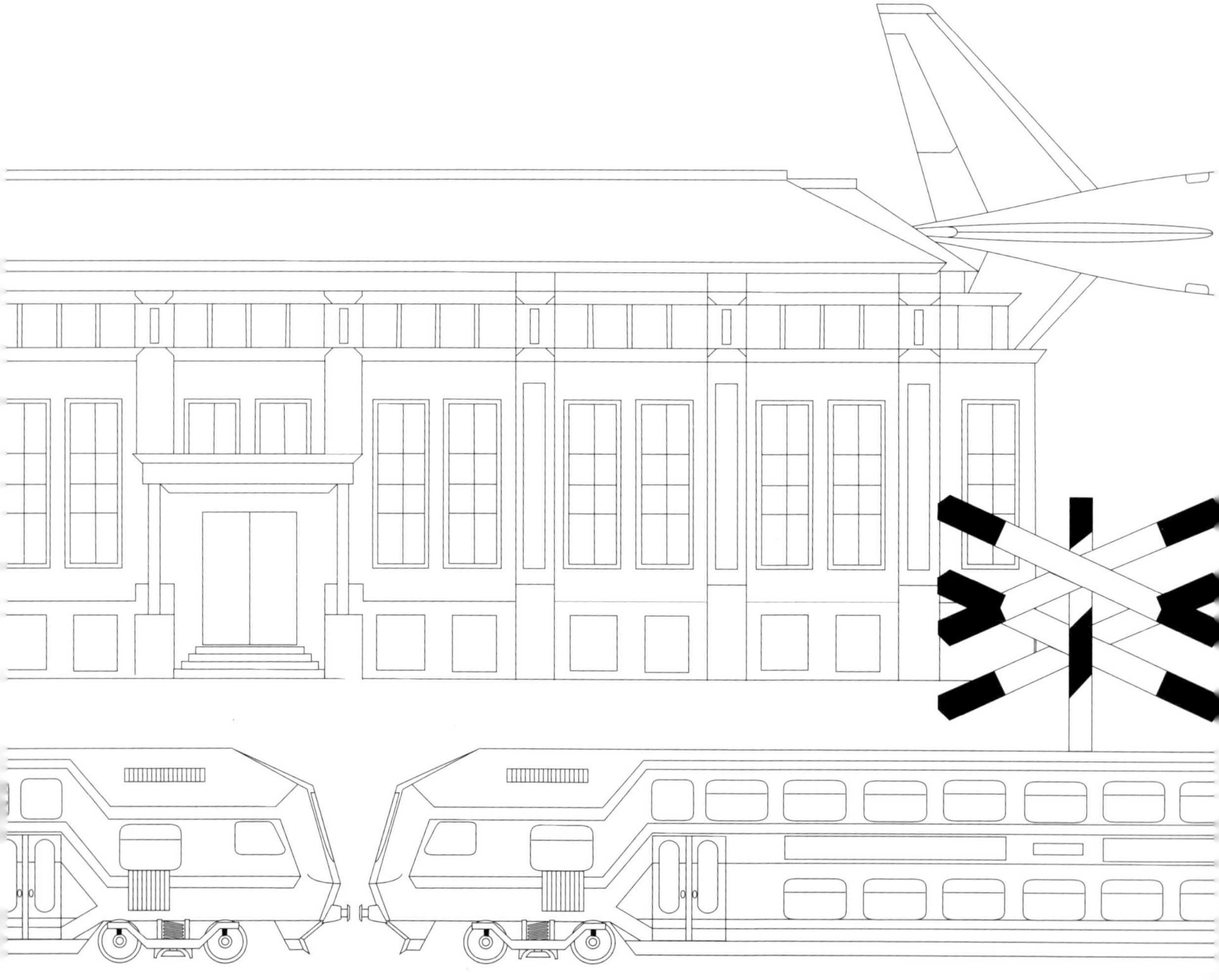

BEYOND AUTOFUNDAMENTALISM

In support of commobility

Henk Oosterling

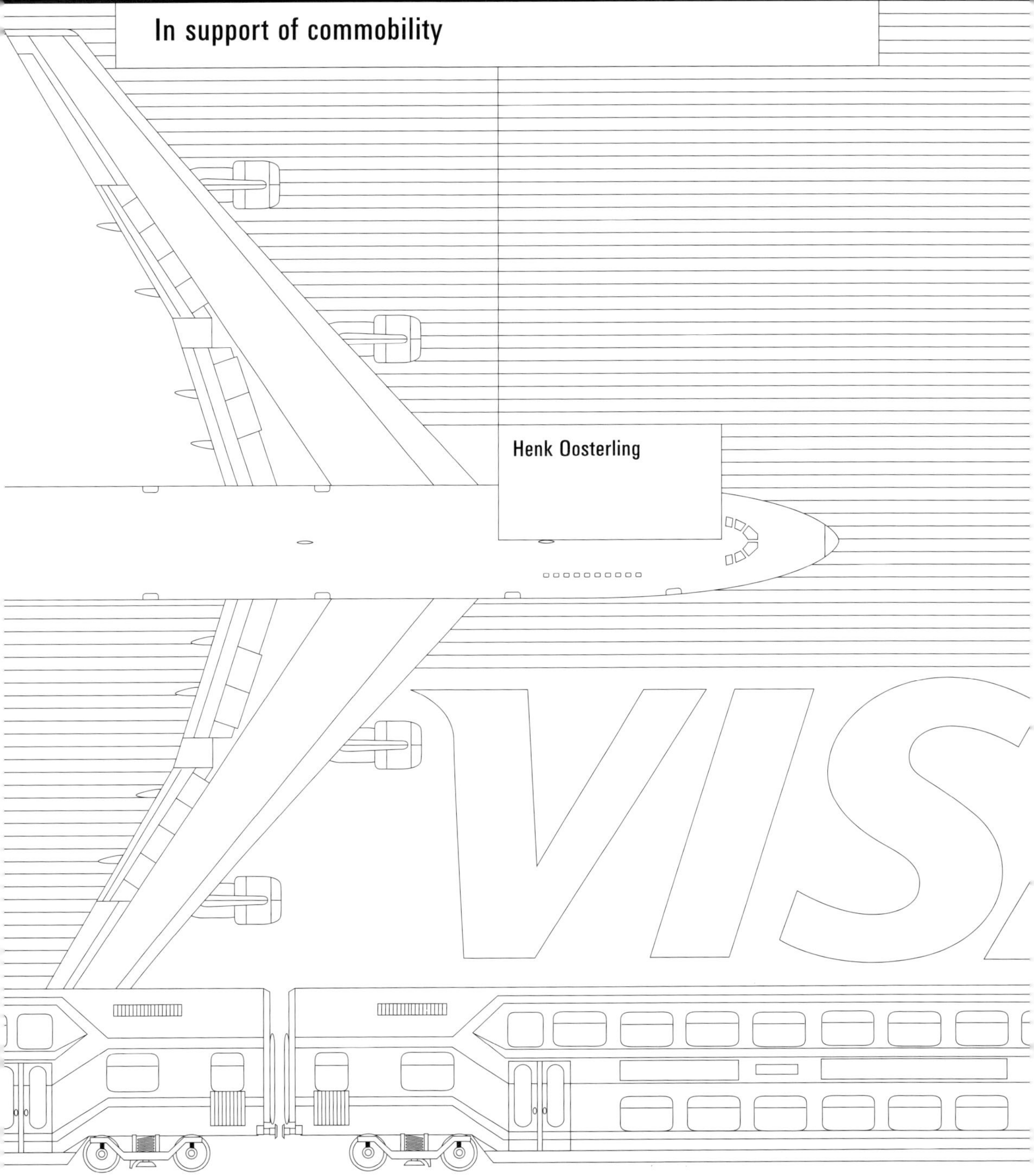

One late Friday afternoon in mid-December a traveller is returning to Rotterdam from a business meeting on Long Island, New York State. Trains are late coming into Penn Station because of a sudden flurry of snowstorms. Connections are missed. Even though the ethereal voices echoing around the rarefied transit space of Newark departure lounge attempt to put the passengers in hopeful mood, the gate numbers and departure times on the screens keep falling behind. Planes have to be de-iced. Arrangements threaten to fall through. The traveller's mobile phone has insufficient range, and he has no telephone card to hand. As the aeroplane glides into the night, the traveller is able to call from the satellite phone sunk into the armrest using his credit card. He sends a few e-mails from his pocket PC with its expandable keyboard. He completes his notes. Meanwhile, the aircraft speeds onward – though seemingly suspended immobile – at more than 900 km/hour towards the other side of the ocean. The traveller follows the intercontinental route still to be covered, step-by-step, on a screen in front of him.

On arriving at Schiphol, the information screens for train arrivals and departures announce that frozen power lines are causing delays on the Amsterdam-Schiphol route. Jetlagged passengers grasp their mobile phones, holding dozy conversations. Most of them are gossiping about sweet nothing while staring blankly in front of them; others are already fully alert and busy relaying the latest state of affairs via their headphones.

At Rotterdam's Central Station the traveller withdraws some euros from the ATM and steps into a waiting taxi. The intercontinental and interlocal congestion acquires a *couleur locale*: they head out into the grips of urban gridlock. Three chock-a-block lanes of cars are being squeezed out of the centre past six sets of traffic lights. Despite the dangerous but well-intended manoeuvres by the Rotterdam chauffeur of Moroccan origin it takes more than a quarter of an hour to get past the Hofplein only 500 metres further on. Their conversation about the practical paradox of 'automobility' – namely the immobilization caused BY the excesses of motorized road travel – is repeatedly interrupted by a voice from the taxi firm's dispatch office. But the chauffeur interweaves his hands-free responses with the conversation, and pointing to a little screen at the bottom of his windscreen he turns the banter to fast and distant journeys: with the Global Positioning System (GPS) it is possible to trace the route to any given street in Helsinki, Moscow or Casablanca. Not only is the car vectorally equipped for the entire globe, but it is also a system that adapts to its driver like a made-to-measure suit: to the left under the dashboard there is a button with three encoded settings, one for each of the taxi's chauffeurs. When one of them keys in his own code the equipment downloads his personal data and the driver's seat adjusts automatically to the most comfortable position for him.

Once out of the centre the journey proceeds smoothly. At the front door, the traveller taps in his access code, walks down the hallway to the waiting lift and whizzes upward. In the bedroom he switches the TV on and zaps through the channels. The adverts urge him to purchase a mobile phone with a built-in camera so he can use MMS, the 'multimedia messaging service'. At any given moment, the owner can telematically share his surroundings with his friends. Exhausted by high-speed stasis and hyperactive observation, the traveller finally falls into a profound slumber.

The car: from status symbol to one of life's essentials

What makes up our modern-day automobility? The answer embraces all the elements mentioned above. We can no longer limit ourselves to inter- and intralocal congestion, unaffordable public transport, the shortage of affordable parking space and more than 1000 traffic deaths per year. The acute problems associated with our automobility cannot simply be solved at a national level with extra taxes, such as the Dutch fuel levy known as the *kwartje van Kok* ('Kok's dimes', after the former Dutch premier who introduced the tax when he was still minister of finance), with bigger speed bumps, wider motorways or more intensive use of carpooling and designating a non-drinking driver to ferry friends home from the bars. Automobility is a universal problem. Like collective consciousness it is integrated in personal visions of life and is a mainstay of daily life. Cars are only a persistent thorn in the side of die-hard 'autophobics' because cars deprive them a view of their unrealistic, foreshortened nostalgic perspective: the car-free village square. For the average mobility consumer, however, cars are an inalienable component of their 'rurban' existence, which traverses countryside (the rural) and city (the urban).

Are they in control of their means of transport or is it taking them for a ride? This line of inquiry presents no viable alternative scenarios. In a world that is replete with mechanical wizardry, transport facilities, communications equipment, pleasure enhancement and narcotics, the means and media – without anyone expressly wanting it – have been a goal in their own right for a long time already. With 'automobility' as a way of life, the distinction between the means and the goal falls by the wayside. Until the 1970s the organization was still fairly easy to grasp. In the Netherlands the car was labelled the 'luxury van'. The car was a personal status symbol and DAF was a national icon.

However, with assembly being spread around the globe, international flows of capital and transfer of production to low-wage countries, the national foundations for the car industry have been swept away. In days gone by, the car was characterized as a basic necessity in the election manifestos of socialist parties. The car and its instrumental value were lost along with the boundary-breaking added value that now attaches itself to excessive indulgence. But at certain times, the phenomenon of 'speeding' raises its head and a pleasure-seeking government minister confesses to having exceeded the speed limit. Motorists want to feel as free as a bird without being labelled an outlaw.

After the Second World War, lifestyling and branding around the car became big business in a Europe focused on mass consumption. In *Mythologies* (1957), Roland Barthes analyses the promotion of the new Citroën DS. This model was 'bought more for its image than as a utilitarian object'. Barthes pointed out the decreasing instrumental value of the car and the emphasis on the interior of the car as private space. The chrome that exudes an impression of control over speed is more indicative of comfort than performance. Design becomes increasingly domestic: 'The dashboard is more like a panel of knobs in a modern kitchen than a switchboard in a factory.' The windows suggest an organic, insect-like 'lightness', the science-fiction seamlessness of the new Citroën DS – *déesse* or goddess – lends it an almost divine sheen.

In the 1970s, via the TV, this representation ended up shifting up a gear. Automobility was increasingly consumed like other products and services in our experience-oriented economy. The car as object became the common ground for experiences associated with active and adventurous lifestyles. The interlocal mass consumption of day-trips, as promoted in the Netherlands by Meta de Vries, radio presenter and jazz singer, were the national pendant of the sequential, international streams of traffic to myriad holiday destinations. This is an automobile-enabled consumption of 'world citizenship' that couples individual freedom of movement with safe and comfortable entertainment. The only geopolitical guarantee for this automobility is a reliable and affordable supply of oil.

The Holy Cow: an autofundamentalist's paradogma

Automobility is a quality of life that can no longer be ignored. For the car-loving fellow citizen, any critique of the car's ubiquity is seen as an anti-emancipatory undermining of the highest values and ideals of modern life: individual autonomy, aesthetic perfection, comfortable privacy, progressive acceleration and unlimited freedom of movement. The active motorist is mirrored in a worldview of the autonomous subject. In turn, this is the modern heir of what Aristotle saw as the cosmic *perpetuum mobile*: God as Prime Mover. The unquestioning worship of the 'Holy Cow' is still a telling reminder of this dogmatic pseudo-religiosity.

Faith in the car is the dynamic paradigm of our orientation to the world. The car as technological miracle and automobility are more than dogmas. For the car-loving majority the demands of a minority to scrap the car are comparable to the repulsive request of asking a healthy person to amputate a leg. The moral repulsion that such a repugnant request would elicit in many people is directly comparable with the resistance that ban on the car arouses among car-owners. Like a self-evident paradogma, automobility buttresses an uncritical defence of car ownership. This 'autofundamentalism' was expressed in a bill, introduced in the Netherlands a few years ago by the VVD (liberal) political party, to include automobility – i.e. car ownership – as a civil right in the constitution.

The paradoxes of automobility

Automobility is a structural component of modern-day Western ambitions. People from the West always want to be going somewhere. In an atheistic society this autonomous individual is no stranger to a certain existential restlessness. But the hyperactivity of modern desire can eventually be traced back to a long tradition full of drive and the desire for renewal, particular to modern politics, science and art. This drive prompts a simple question: *where* is it that these automobile people are heading exactly? Do they want to get from A to B as comfortably, safely and efficiently as possible? One glimpse of a morning rush hour or the city centre during the weekend immediately belies this.

Clearly something else is going on. The pleasure of driving for the sake of driving – from Sunday day-trippers to joyriders – still plays a role, but more important is the availability of a car. This holds a promise of free self-determination, of autonomy – we can, after all, head off whenever we desire. The promise that automobile readiness holds is reiterated in political manifestos, academic tracts, technological predictions and economic projections, and it is practised in parliament, courts of law, the wage-setting negotiations of Social and Economic Councils, and museums. The self-critical individual with his freedom of choice and self-determination is the canonic law.

In its excesses, however, this auto- (Greek: *autos*) mobility (Latin: *mobilis*) holds striking paradoxes. Individual freedom in a traffic jam or in the dynamic hunt for a parking space – driving round and round to spy out a parking space – soon turns into collective captivity. On an ethical level, where it is a question of life and death, these paradoxes are even more obvious: from the 'right to terminate a pregnancy' to the right to terminate one's own life, the individual who enjoys self-determination is empowered – no matter what the quality of an individual life – to end a life with a single gesture, even his or her own life. Unlike the motivation of Palestinian suicide bombers this is about the quality of one's own life. The impossibility of reversing the ecologically catastrophic impact of massive car use through international cooperation is indicative of a similarly paradoxical logic on the level of automobility.

Does this self-destructive logic tally with the image of the enlightened modern-day individuals? Answering this inevitably requires a consideration of cultural history. The fact is that the modern enlightenment process – collective and individual emancipation and a critical awakening – has an 'invisible' complement: sensory enlightenment. This involves increasing the sensitization of our sensorial machinery. In *Understanding Media* (1966), Marshall McLuhan interprets technological tools or media as extensions of our physical functions. He points out that every medium creates its own environment. If this becomes a quality in and of itself then the medium is the message. The achievements of this sensory enlightenment are then just as difficult to reverse as the critical awakening that the Enlightenment is invariably reduced to.

Physical enlightenment: acceleration

Sensory enlightenment has a physical and a visual component. In physical enlightenment (en-*lighten*-ment) we strive, through acceleration, towards the relief of physical discomfort. Walking is more tiring and riding a motorbike is chillier than driving in a car with air conditioning. Since the late eighteenth century, individuals have travelled more comfortably and rapidly in steam trains; somewhat later in passenger cars and private planes. Uplifting a 'burdened' body brings on an ecstatic sensation. As to the question of whether we can imagine a society that denies the body in the same way the soul was denied earlier, Paul Virilio's answer in *L' horizon négatif* (1984) is that this is the society that we are heading toward. In his analysis of the relationships between power, trans-port and acceleration he concludes that the secret of every hegemony is based on an ideal weightlessness.

Physical enlightenment was fulfilled with the first flight to the moon. The Apollo astronaut floated in a vacuum. Televisual humankind was granted its first glimpse of the globe. The victory over gravity extended the onward march of visual surveillance. For the astronaut speed is a function of an unadulterated observation of points and planes. In *Mythologies*, Roland Barthes announced the advent of this 'jet-man' as the beginning of a new era in aviation, with a pilot who is more robot than hero. The jet-man voluntarily becomes one with 'his' machine and media: in his autonomous struggle for weightlessness the pilot, paradoxically enough, places his autonomy in the 'hands' of technology. He subjugates himself to the level of the means. Faith in himself equals an absolute trust in the technology surrounding him. He is no hero, but actually mediocre in his absolute faith in a total and machine-driven functionality within an all-encompassing technological system. This autofundamentalistic trust is indicative of the crypto-religious character of an ecstatic automobility.

Visual enlightenment: transparent surveillance

As a mediocre being, the jet-man is connected to the world via visual representations on an interface. Physical enlightenment is coupled with visual enlightenment in the same way. Cars, mobile phones and modems are inextricably linked. A BMW without a mobile phone or GPS, without information or communications technology, is inconceivable. Campfires, candles and oil lamps delivered humankind from darkness in pre-modern times, the discovery of electricity and the invention of electric light, telephones and television prepared the way for the digital revolution, and now it is the turn of computer-controlled vehicles. The 'jalopy' is exchanged for the mobile phone that then logs in with a technoscape. Once lit by lampposts, the public domain is now illuminated by enormous flatscreens and millions of displays. Previously unknown public spaces are opening up, from virtual plaza to digital cities.

Transportation cannot manage without technology, and streams of traffic are unmanageable without a technological infrastructure. Every form of transport is like an information-packed cell and an interactive interface, connected to computers fed by satellites. Every automobile movement – whether a car, a mobile phone or a mobile SCUD missile – can be traced using GPS. Beings that are not logged in or are located in remote corners beyond the reach of antennae can be traced to within a square metre by spy satellites. The physical automobility of individuals is increasingly dictated by this all-seeing surveillance.

This affects well-travelled world citizens as well as funshoppers, escaped pets and lost children, repeat offenders and the infirm dependent on extramural care. Cash flow starts with a chip-bearing bankcard, the first chip has been inserted into a child in England in order to prevent kidnap and the electronic tagging of convicts sitting sentences out at home is already standard practice. While motorists use the car to purchase cigarettes at the shop on the corner, pensioners go shopping via the Internet. They do their banking from home, call for the home help using a central alarm service, or they SMS and MMS with their grandchildren in Australia. They virtually speed around the globe. The criterion for their automobility is not horsepower, but the speed of light in which visual transparency (light) and material enlightenment (speed) coincide.

Critical insight, material release and visual overview come together in automobilization. Critical assessment does not prevent automobile behaviour, but legitimizes it. After all, were the critical consciousness of the negative effects the decisive factor, then many of the motorists would have given up their cars already.

Capsular consciousness and radical mediocrity

The fact that this does not happen does not, moreover, mean that the flesh is weaker than the mind. It hints that sensory and spiritual enlightenment share a common point of orientation: the autonomy and inviolability of the interior, the inner life. This is seen as the private domain. In modern society, inner life is culturally moulded into white cubes and black boxes for the sake of 'civilization': museums, concert halls and theatres cultivate the sensibility of their visitors rather than encourage critical reflection. Physical contact is avoided: the light is still dimmed, people hardly communicate and touching is taboo. These hyperindividual sensibilities have a cultural legitimacy. However, this self-gratification has something narcissistic and anti-social about it. This becomes clear when the automobile throw themselves into the public sphere with their 'capsular' consciousness. In order to avoid being physically exposed to the public sphere they encapsulate themselves in cars and mobile phones. Just like an owner-occupied house, these physical and virtual capsules are bolted shut with codes and passwords. This is how the automobile radius of action branches out from the private domain: the car sprays domestic security, warmth, safety and comfort into the public domain on all sides, and with the mobile phone the caller draws in this domesticity more closely. Fitting cars with information and communication technologies and implanting the mobile phone in public space means that the automobilists actually never leave their homes. While staring their fellow travellers straight in the face they are on stand-by via an interface or an earpiece. This sustains the illusion that automobilists, making their own decisions and moving as they will, are kings of their own castles, more pilot than passenger, more driver than fellow traveller. Constricted by safety belts they are something like the completely paralysed physicist Stephen Hawking, famous for his attempts to sum up the fundamental forces of the universe in a single denominator. Just like Hawking, they are not a 'ghost in the machine' but 'ghost as the machine'. They are no longer independent or superior to their means and media; they are now right in the middle. By building themselves into their media or implanting these media in themselves, their sense of reality and personal experience has gradually taken on the parameters of 'their' means.

Time and space orientation of individuals seem to be dependent on the medium used. Every means has its own measure. For example, car-owners denied their cars become just as disoriented and uprooted as anyone who has his TV confiscated, his telephone cut off, or finds his server is suddenly down. It is only when they no longer function that means of transport and communications media are appreciated as more than just convenient tools. On penalty of otherwise having to consider the users as addicts, when we lack these tools we must recognize that they are life's indispensable essentials. The automobilist turns out to be radically mediocre.

Public transport: from autofundamentalism to commobility

Thus far, an involuntary distinction has been made between the car-owners, users of public transport and home-based teleworkers. However, with no beating around the bush, as regards the phenomenon of automobility the distinction between these groups is becoming increasingly blurred. The private-public polarity has in fact worn very quickly. Mobility consumers travelling in public may be caught in delays, but they are more virtually mobile and communicative than ever before, while automobilists end up ever more immobilized but are as manoeuvrable as their public transport counterparts. On closer consideration they are all home-workers.

At a given moment, the distinction will become so minimal that the refusal to give up the car will take on explicitly autofundamentalistic proportions, because reality itself will have dissolved the antithesis. In future, the government will be solving mobility paradoxes using a GPS-controlled traffic management system on motorways fitted with sensors. In fact a car fully stowed with sensors will then be dynamically parked in a column of automobiles. It is only possible to maintain the illusion of driving in residential areas. But these are filled with speed bumps. Mobile traffic jams will move onward on sensorized motorways. Finally, this immobilized mobility foreshadows the ultimate paradox of the manipulative automobile subject: hands-free driving in an immobilized automobility.

All this will no more detract from the car-driver's sense of freedom than does camera surveillance in public spaces. The more communication and information media are integrated in an automobile capsule, the more free and safe people feel. Eventually they will be as free, autonomous and safe as their teleworking and train-using counterparts. On the level of personal experience, the capsule presents automobilists a knotted experience of themselves: everything comes together in their ears and eyes and they are sitting at the controls. But from a radically mediocre viewpoint, this capsular consciousness is a vacuous midpoint that pulsates at the level of the means and the media. It is an intersection in a web spun from physical and virtual threads. The automobilist is a crossroads incarnate. As soon as we extrapolate this idea, the capsular consciousness itself proves to be a transit space that messages whisk through. If we inquire into the quality of the public domain and the nature of this new public space, we come up with a startling answer: the private has become completely public. Automobility is first and foremost mobility with others: commobility.

This seems to bring the argument to a close in favour of public transport. Why would we not face up to the inevitable consequences of our excessive automobility and create space for advanced and free publicness? Why would we proscribe the notion that the perceived lack of safety on the streets is probably caused, in part, by reduction of the public domain to a sum of vacuous private domains that only use the public space for shopping and to transmit messages? Admittedly, a post-automobile existence is an unthinkable option. But as long as we continue, in our radical mediocrity, to identify our 'selves' with 'auto' and while this is the 'medium' as 'message', we will not get much further in our thinking about mobility in relation to the public space. The safety and vitality of the public space probably has more to gain from smashing open the capsule and propagating public participation and interested – as the condition of the in-between, the 'esse' of the 'inter' – interactions.

LANDMARKS

The image of the city of Rotterdam is to a large extent defined and coloured by its traffic infrastructure. Parts of this infrastructure are the most remarkable landmarks in Rotterdam.

Dolf Broekhuizen

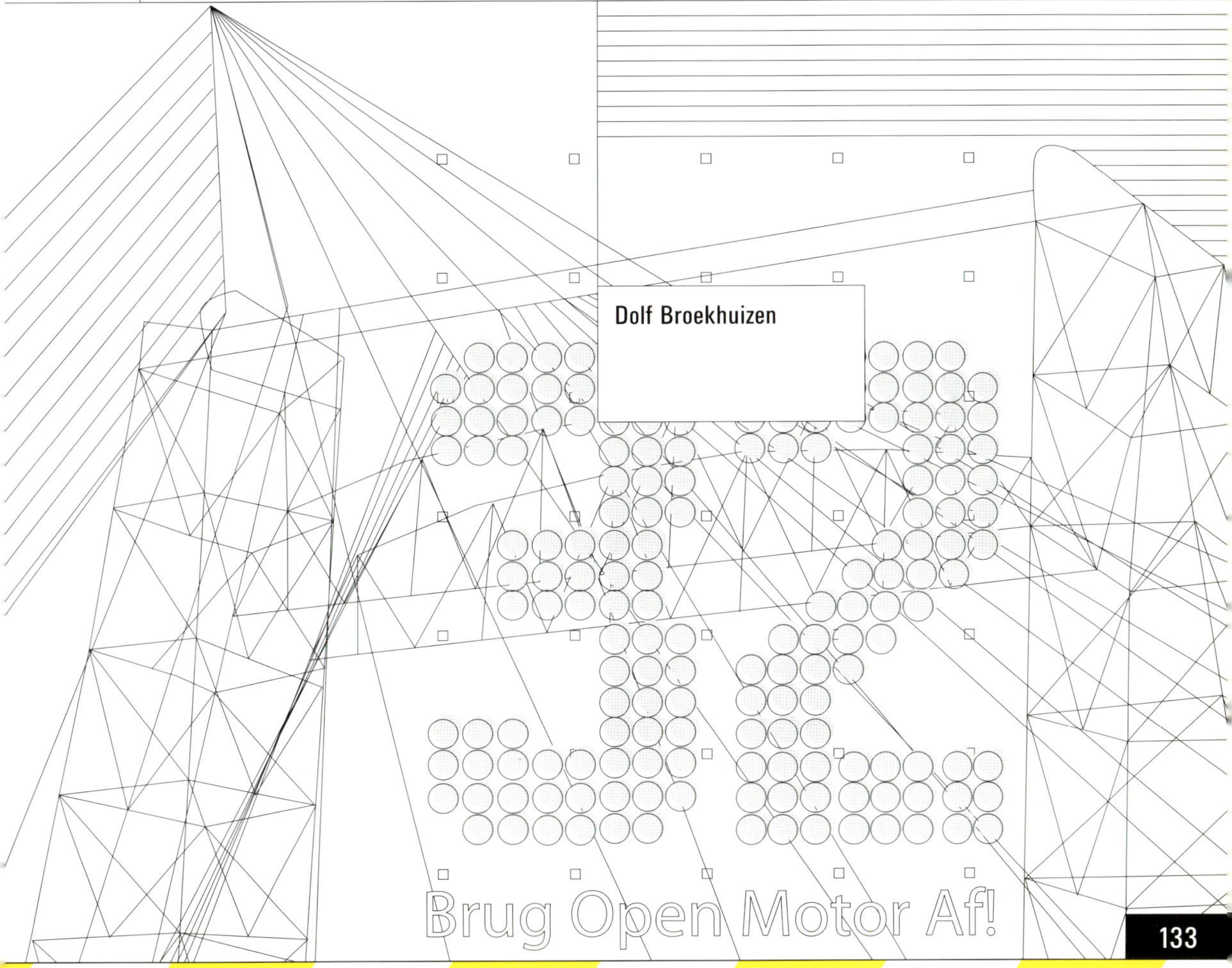

Maas Tunnel

At its opening in 1942, the Maas Tunnel represented a summation of engineering innovations. This first automobile tunnel in the Netherlands was intended to relieve the existing cross-Maas ferries and the permanent river crossing over the Noordereiland for city and regional traffic. The tunnel consisted of two two-lane conduits for through traffic and two smaller conduits, positioned one on top of the other, for cyclists and pedestrians. In a separate building, emergency vehicles stood ready to tow broken-down cars quickly out of the tunnel. The Maas Tunnel was the tail end of a partially subterranean motorway over the 's-Gravendijkwal embankment, which channels automobile traffic via single-level and flyover junctions through the city. The beautifully designed entrance buildings and the escalator for pedestrians and cylcists were no less of a sensation at the time. Two towering ventilation structures, designed by then city architect, Ad van der Steur, marked the tunnel entrance on either side of the Maas. This made the complex, viewed from the water and from outside the tunnel, a symbol of speed and modernity that stirred the imagination.

Caland Canal Windbreak

The windbreak built along the Caland Canal in the late 1980s stands on an inhumanly large scale. The 1,700-metre-long colossus is built out of concrete elements 25 metres high. The wind barrier was built for the container ships piloted through the narrow passageway at the Caland Bridge by tugboats. In southerly and easterly winds above force 5 on the Beaufort scale, it was impossible for these ships to sail past the bridge: their relatively lightweight and tall construction would cause them to be blown against the bridge. The windbreak cuts the wind force by an average of 2 on the Beaufort scale. Architect Maarten Struys created the design. The round and square shapes are an allusion to the storage tanks and containers characteristic of the Botlek and Europoort docks.

Centraal Station

Rotterdam's Central Station, either from the front or from the rear, is positioned prominently at the end of a green axis – the Westersingel and the Spoorsingel, respectively. On the side facing the city centre especially, this location is exploited to make a monumental statement. Architect Sybolt van Ravenstein designed the station, opened in 1957, as an orderly, elongated building. The facades of the main hall in the centre and offices in the side wings form one wall of the Stationsplein. The slightly curved facade reinforces the bowl-shaped space of the square, where buses, taxis and trams ride up to the station entrance. Traffic crossing through from the Weena is diverted along an underpass and so does not disrupt the relationship with the green axis of the Westersingel. The *singel*, or canal promenade, has recently been upgraded with sculptures. Travellers arriving in Rotterdam by train get a monumental view of the city through a large window spanning the full breadth and height of the station hall.

Maas Boulevard

Because dock activities began a steady exodus from the old city centre in 1900, the Maas is no longer the important shipping lane for goods transport it once was. The river and the dock basins are being assigned other functions. In the city centre, the water is the largest public space for the redevelopment of the residential, employment and recreational functions along the riverbanks. This can be readily experienced along the Maas Boulevard. This boulevard was built on a former railway embankment in the 1950s. Coming from the Oostelijke Ringweg (Eastern Ringroad), motorists driving into the city via the Maas Boulevard are presented with a gorgeous panorama of Rotterdam in a single all-encompassing picture. At the Boompjes, a wharf that was redesigned in 1989, an esplanade gives emphatic shape to the contact with the river. This design by the firms of OMA, Cees Christiaanse, Bureau B+B and Rotterdam's own Department for Urban Planning, Housing and Traffic (dS+V) assigns a great deal of space to recreation, including an events area on the embankment and a jogging path along the wharf.

Erasmus Bridge

Ever since it was opened in 1996, the Erasmus Bridge has been the symbolic heart of contemporary Rotterdam and an eye-catching trademark in the city's silhouette. The bridge, designed by Ben van Berkel, consists of a graceful light-blue pylon, from which a slender carriageway hangs suspended. The bridge's construction underscores an ambition to expand the city centre across the river. The city authorities made a conscious choice in 1991 for a relatively expensive, image-defining design, which would give significant impetus to the shift of the centre across the river. The suspension bridge's asymmetrical pylon, inclined toward the south, symbolizes the 100-year-old, distorted relationship in development of the city between its north and south banks, which had to be set right with a single gesture. The Erasmus Bridge is the perfect embodiment of the 'leap across the river'.

Kleinpolderplein

The Kleinpolderplein dates from a period in which the Netherlands had few motorway interchanges. Compared to other, later traffic interchanges along the *Ruit van Rotterdam* (the 'Rotterdam Diamond', a reference to the rhomboid pattern formed by four motorways ringing the city), what stands out is how extremely compact the Kleinpolderplein is. When the first two ovoid traffic loops were built in 1951, this was still a roundabout of sizeable dimensions. After the subterranean underpass and the two-storey-high flyovers were added around 1963, it became clear that the bends were far too sharp and provided insufficient sightlines for a traffic interchange of this scale. Oil drums were placed in the curves to cushion any lorries that might miscalculate them. What is exceptional is that the urban buildings of the Kleinpolder are not set apart from the motorway, but instead stand right next to it, and even have their own access points to the interchange, for through traffic as well as for slower traffic. This is because the district, which is cut in half by the road connection to The Hague, was already under construction when the first sketches for the interchange were committed to paper.

The Lift Bridge

The Lift Bridge ('Hefbrug' in Dutch), from its construction in 1928 until the opening of the railway tunnel in 1993, was part of Rotterdam's 'aerial railway' – an elevated railway that ran through the city centre, over the Maas and the Noordereiland to the south. Rail traffic rode right through the city, free of obstructions from other city traffic. Only barge traffic on the Maas had to be reckoned with. The metal lift bridge designed by P. Joosting replaced an 1877 revolving railway bridge. This proud feat of engineering quickly became a symbol for Rotterdam after it was built, thanks in part to it having been filmed by Joris Ivens. The exceptional construction with two lift towers formed a beacon in the city and a symbol for the link between the city centre on the north bank and the working-class neighbourhoods on the south bank. After the railway tunnel became operational, the aerial railway became defunct and was dismantled. Only the two lift towers with the bridge section in the open position were retained. The symbol of Rotterdam as an industrial city became a congealed reminder, redundant.

Wilhelminaplein

Traffic over the Erasmus Bridge emerges onto the Wilhelminaplein, which serves as a pivotal junction for traffic flowing between South and North Rotterdam. The square is an important orientation point on the Kop van Zuid and forms the continuation of the central city axis from the Hofplein and the Coolsingel. On what was once a dockland, an expansion of the city centre began to emerge in 1990. The public space of the square has been painstakingly laid out. Subtle details like specially developed sand-hued paving stones and a square pattern of red-and-white pedestrian crossings are indicative of the new significance of the square to the city. One of the most important elements of the Wilhelminaplein is the square's open wall on the riverside. Here a beautiful wharf with a belvedere, designed by Peter Wilson, provides a view onto the square as well as onto the banks of the Maas.

Van Brienenoord Bridge

Anyone driving toward Rotterdam from the south sees the Van Brienenoord Bridge rise above the landscape in the distance. From the bridge one gets a wide view over the Maas River, with the urban landscape of Rotterdam on either side. This is the special way in which the arched bridge marks the entrance to Rotterdam. Keeping the characteristic shape of the bridge was an important point of consideration for its expansion in 1990. To address greater mobility, the old bridge, designed by builder W. van der Eb, was not torn down to make way for an entirely new, bigger and up-to-date river crossing. Instead, the capacity of the original 1965 bridge was doubled by building a second arch. This new section of the bridge, set right next to the original bridge arch, is a little wider but otherwise virtually identical. This intervention reinforces the Van Brienenoord Bridge's function as an effective means of stage-managing the landscape.

Hofplein

The Hofplein, which before the 1940 bombardment had been a bone of contention because of frequent traffic snarl-ups, evolved during the Reconstruction into an efficient traffic intersection and a centre of urban life. The Reconstruction Structural Plan (1946) designated the square as the starting point of a modern city axis, running via the Coolsingel to the 'window on the river'. In the centre of the Hofplein stands a monumental fountain with carvings representing the city's position on the Maas. Once such international firms as Shell and Hilton opened premises on the Hofplein, the reputation of the new heart of the city was assured. The high-rises around the square eclipsed the dominance of the Sint Laurens tower and the city hall tower in the city silhouette. Even though the Hilton has moved its entrance to the Kruiskade and Shell has left, the Hofplein has maintained its role in the heart of the city. The square is the centre of public celebrations of important events.

strepen
trekken

MAKING SPACE FOR MOBILITY

Pieter Schrijnen

Accounts of mobility, of movement and travel, and of the societal significance of mobility are usually told by spatial planners, designers and culture aficionados. All the same, it is traffic experts, working on a more practical level, who play the biggest role in the planning and design of infrastructure and intersections. Even though traffic and transport are so important for the dynamics of society, spatial planning really has little grip on it. Spatial planners and designers of traffic and transport have their own respective perspective on the city and region and make their own contributions to its development, as mapped out here. This article also examines how these two disciplines can contribute to the spatial quality of city and region.
The line of thought behind this text is derived from the theory of the learning organization and experiences with innovation processes related to traffic and transport. In short, social quality, like substantive renewal, is seldom the work of a single discipline. The interaction between people from different disciplines plays a guiding role. The organization of the work process has considerable impact on the outcomes of the planning. Breaking free of sector interests and working from a context of common values fosters that interaction. On the basis of trust and mutual commitment, project teams in which disciplines come together can produce exceptional things. This essay considers a number of substantive, procedural and contextual break-throughs, which in Rotterdam have led to projects of compelling allure for the city and region.

Special infrastructure projects

Anyone in Rotterdam discussing projects with genuine allure mentions the Kop van Zuid. Indeed, the project (regeneration of the port area on the southern banks of the Maas) boasts an exceptional history. There was no clear-cut brief for this area, along the lines of 'make the Kop van Zuid'.
What there was, for the most part, were problems: antiquated and polluted docklands, social and economic conflicts between the northern and southern banks of the Maas, with the river as a physical barrier between the two parts of the city. The area is now part of the city centre, with space for offices, facilities and housing in attractive surroundings. The Kop van Zuid plays a role in the city's recreational and cultural activities. A new urban artery, a metro station and a tramline link it all with the surrounding city.
These developments are the result of a special work process within the Rotterdam City Council. The project started from the notion that new infrastructure, in the form of the construction of the second city bridge, could serve as leverage to turn the numerous problems into oppor-tunities. The infrastructure linked the various challenges and gave the area's image substantial impetus. Remarkably, these opportunities lay not primarily in the area of traffic, but rather at the level of the city as a whole. They related the socio-economic development of Zuid to the expansion of the city centre and the way in which the city is positioned along the river. Once these potentialities were understood, the project's goals and strategy became clear. To capi-talize on these opportunities, the various sectors really needed one another, which the city authorities and the management of the city services used as a guiding principle for cooperation between all the departments and

individuals involved. And it worked. Neither the traffic sector nor any of the other sectors worked on resolving only its own problems. On the con-trary, they worked systematically on the social and cultural essence van de project: the city-wide challenge. This project placed strong emphasis on the design quality of the bridge and the metro station. The result was a recognizable identity so powerful that de Erasmus Bridge has actually become the city's trademark.

The Benelux Line project – an extension of the metro network in a westerly direction – shows comparable points of interface, though this project was developed in a different way. It began with Rijkswaterstaat (the Directorate-General for Public Works and Water Management) and its intention to build the second Benelux Tunnel to accommodate the increasing of capacity on the A4 motorway. It proved financially and procedurally attractive to simultaneously construct a metro tunnel. The east-west line could thus be extended, and Spijkenisse, via Hoogvliet, Vlaardingen and Schiedam, was connected with the Rotterdam city centre.

The long collaboration between the City Council's experts, Rotterdam's public transport company (RET) and Rijkswaterstaat has resulted in a mutual recognition of the national, regional and metropolitan interests at stake. The decision to build the metro line was therefore agreed to quite quickly. For a project of this size, this is remarkable in itself. This consensus also created the confidence not to have traffic expertise and civil engineering take the lead in designing the line. It was entrusted instead to urban planners and architects. They were asked to introduce something unique within the rural and urban environment. This approach was followed in introducing the line into its rural and urban settings, both in terms of location and connection to the surroundings. With its stop on the Benelux Line, the Schiedam station gained a new position in the region's spatial planning structure. The cities of Schiedam and Rotterdam used this as a basis for the joint Schieveste project, which aims to build offices and facilities at this new junction.

The project can mean renewed impetus for the faltering development of Schiedam and Rotterdam-West. This rests on two breakthroughs: an attractive transport hub has been designed, and the two neighbouring city governments are prepared to join forces in regenerating this urban area. The mental image of a 'big' Rotterdam looking down on its 'little' neighbour Schiedam has been jettisoned. Here too the need for urban renewal provided a common context.

The success of such projects is no accident, but neither is it inevitable. Projects such as the Kop van Zuid or Schieveste call for the development and constant safeguarding of a common vision, which transcends the conflicts between various parties. Each party has a tendency to put its own interests first, to use the money available primarily for its own solutions. Over-coming these conflicts comes by no means naturally to the traffic experts or the urban planners.

The traffic projects

The transport networks do not dictate people's behaviour. Traffic models are primarily based on the economic considerations of people in transit. These can be made 'concrete', quantified, illustrated. The social and cultural aspects of mobility are more difficult to capture. Mobile people constantly exploit the available networks in new ways. It is not easy to predict which places prove attractive, how people travel and in which proportions car, bike and public transport are used. The spatial and economic dynamics of city and region are also almost impossible to predict.

Traffic experts are constantly adapting networks to this barely predictable dynamic. Their most important partners often have economic interests at stake, such as the Port Authority, transport concerns, shipping companies and real-estate investors. The transport networks must also provide access to new residential areas and industrial estates, preferably in a way free of nuisance complaints for existing residents and users.

The traffic expert aims to succeed in such as aspects as accessibility and circulation; his or her essential challenge is 'to make the machine go'. Moreover, the traffic expert is oriented toward improving safety and reducing nuisance complaints. Often long-term projects with highly specific interest groups are involved. The work often prompts resistance in the city – it creates a great deal of disruption. Not only motorways, but also TramPlus projects involve conflict between public and individual interests. The traffic expert traditionally focuses more on systems than on people. Discussions are often about the means, far more rarely about the social challenge at hand. The financial backers, most often higher-level government authorities, have explicit sector objectives. Within the city government there is a specific alderman for traffic and close lines of communication with the traffic departments of neighbouring municipalities, the region and the Ministry of Transport, Public Works and Water Management. The city's Ontwikkelingsbedrijf Rotterdam (Rotterdam City Development Corporation, or OBR) maintains close ties with the traffic experts, because a direct link is being made between investments in transport infrastructure and property developments. For the extensive port area, a comparable relationship exists with the Gemeentelijk Havenbedrijf Rotterdam (Rotterdam Municipal Port Management, or GHR). The projects there often have a utilitarian character, for which a sector approach is adequate.

For decades, huge investments were made in new infrastructure. Now the focus is on improved exploitation of the existing network, including the application of engineering, telematics and traffic management. Factors such as travel comfort, the pleasure of moving through city and region are getting attention. There is a clear shift toward a broader perspective. Traffic experts are increasingly asked to contribute an integrated product. However, the sector decision-making circuits and cash flows hardly oriented toward this. They measure things on the basis of figures and sector criteria. Calculations remain an important activity for a traffic manager.

The urban planning project

For urban planners, their clients are first and foremost the people and the culture of the city, even though it is the city council that formally issues a commission. The urban planner focuses on the spatial integration all manner of sector initiatives, on the social and cultural challenges, on the people in the city. Rotterdam must be an attractive city to live in, to work in or to visit.

People must feel that they like being here, want to stay here and will come back here. The region's 1.2 million inhabitants are proud of the city, even though there is a whole load of tensions and they complain a lot. This attitude on the part of their 'clients' motivates the urban planners. Rotterdam holds particular appeal for urban planners, because of the city's multicultural population, because of the inhabitants' pride in their city and the port. The open culture is gaining in fame: 'The people of Rotterdam welcome new contributions. Here you are challenged and here people listen to you.'

The work of the urban planner consists of the functional and organizational layout of areas. Design is intensely emphasized. It entails the experience of users and residents, the development of identity, of a character that suits the location of the project, of that area in the structure of city and region. Finally, urban development plans make it possible to create space for housing, companies, facilities and other functions. Working to gather support has only recently become a prerequisite of a project. This means the support of people in other fields of expertise, but also the support of authorities and city residents. The management of the city's Department for Urban Planning, Housing and Traffic (dS+V) assesses plans and ideas for their value in regard to reality, as well as their feasibility, support and political importance.

The first tool for urban planning is the ability to make a diagnosis. Then one needs to create feasible and desirable visions for the future, and visualize them. Knowledge of the programme, of the actors, of plan outlines and legislation also plays a background role. Then comes the enthusiasm, the ability of people to learn from and inspire one another. It involves skills such as listening and putting curiosity and equality to use, as well as pro-active communication with management, with the managements of other departments, with the authorities.

Urban planning generates hardly any money of its own. The urban planners are therefore dependent on the investments of other parties and on subsidies, especially from the state. The character and the quality of the plans often dictate the size of the investments. Urban planning proposals must primarily rely on their capacity to convince, their capacity to appeal to and seduce other parties. Working with maps, images and stories is a big part of this.

These differences in context and methodologies mean there are substantive differences between projects relating to infrastructure policy and urban planning projects. The traffic experts often work for other commissioning entities and have other clients. They have their own sector-based contacts with public officials, their own coalitions and their own sources of funding. Their projects have a different reach; a different community judges their work. This means that cooperation is not a given. Fine-tuning issues are more rule than exception.

These differences are not limited to the traffic and urban planning sectors. Such observations can also be made on the environmental, parks, economy and public housing sectors. The traffic sector is no exception within the broad arena of spatial planning. This means the challenge is always to bring and hold together these divergent interests and perspectives.

What is the secret of successful projects, in which the traffic and urban planning cultures reinforce and complement? One precondition for success is a management and government that form a multiple commissioning entity, working toward an integrated vision. The arguments to support the vision and strategy must not come from one field of expertise. A project based on sector-oriented tasks (traffic circulation, environmental nuisance abatement, construction of a particular number of dwellings) undermines the synergy between the disciplines. Projects that solve a problem are essentially different to projects that create value. Argumentation should originate from social, cultural and economic challenges for the city and region.

The climate 'at the top' determines the power of a project team to a large degree. In practice, this is not always positive. Sometimes there is no cooperation at all; sometimes it only happens by coincidence. Managers and administrators who operate from their own area of expertise contribute less to the synergy than those whose work is based on the social challenge faced by city and region. Spanners in the works are those people or departments putting their own little fiefdoms first. These are people who look at projects strictly from the viewpoint of their own values and standards, who refuse to commit themselves to a common vision, to a social project for the city. Someone who puts his expertise or personal solutions first is also a bad team player. In a culture not oriented toward cooperation, a project team degenerates into autonomic roles and segregated responsibilities. Adhering to a formal division of roles hinders synergy. One effective way of creating cooperation is to judge and stimulate professionals based on their substantive input, as well as to invest in cooperation, communication and coaching. That can only benefit the projects and the city.

Money is rarely a stumbling block, despite the eternal lack of it. When the process proceeds smoothly a project can create value and attract money. Money only becomes a problem if investors gauge it according to their own goals and fail to commit themselves to the overriding task at hand. It is a general rule that parties whose sole function is to assess create stumbling blocks. 'The power of obstacles' and directives create no value.

Environmental aspects, for example, are often stumbling blocks. The traffic sector is significantly hobbled by this. Moreover, evaluation shows that actual impact or perceived impact is not proportional to the strict character of legal guidelines. There could be much more room to produce cohesive designs. Flexibility in setting standards can provide room for new forms of urbanism around nodes and lines of infrastructure.

The culture of Rotterdam is oriented toward cooperation. In general this results in good products. Yet it is often a struggle; cooperation does not happen by itself. Not every project gets the room for an open exploration, for that synergy. Not every urban planner or traffic expert has the skills to generate open cooperation. That is why they often meet each other in a setting in which individual interests and roles predominate over the opportunities for city and region.

Urban planners traditionally consider themselves to a large extent responsible for the synergy between areas of expertise. In reality they of course do this from their own perspective on the city and on the character of the projects.

Every discipline active in the broad arena van de spatial planning, however, contributes to this development of the city and region. The form of the cooperation determines what social returns on investments the plans generate. There lies the crux. When the operating process allows for equal input from all fields of expertise and parties, it provides all its participants with a context for synergy.

Integrating planning processes

In the setting of Rotterdam a number of operational forms have proved effective. These operational forms are not yet a given for all projects, but they have shown their usefulness.
The context, again, is the commission. It most often involved multiple projects, which is why it is crucial that the commissioning parties are of one mind, trust one another, and clearly define the task at hand. This also applies to the various managers and the various administrators. When different government entities work together, whether the administrators are prepared to learn from each other or are prepared to support each other's interests and projects is always a question mark.
A project without problems or opportunities leads to an operating process that bonds no one. Projects call for a shared sense of urgency and clear opportunities. This urgency must be recognized by political and market parties. That also attracts money. A plan also requires a strategy, not just scale models. The vision to be developed should provide an answer to this. This vision transcends the sectors and has a bonding effect. A project with a social or cultural character is more conducive to this than a sector-based project.
The beginnings of projects set the tone for cooperation. Starting with a dialogue makes it palpable that there is room for all the contributions, intuitions and unresolved issues. Respect for all the contributions creates a bond between the people who will be working together. It is also extremely effective to alternate perspectives, to focus on each input in turn and work out all of its implications. By taking other parties seriously, one can also involve another in one's work. This creates trust. Involving management in this dialogue also creates commitment.
An interesting example of a methodology that creates openness and commitment was that of the regional plan, a few years ago. Administrators in the neighbouring cities and boroughs were posed four 'life questions':
Who are you now, what is going on in your municipality?
Who do you actually want to be or become?
What are your most important problems?
What are the biggest tasks and how do all these plans contribute to them?
The 'wishy-washy' character of these questions raised some eyebrows, yet in every case they led to genuine discussions about identity and values. These discussions made it possible to arrive at a number of common projects and at an acknowledgement of the diversity of the projects for the individual participants. This provided a context of commitment for the work on the regional plans. These questions can lay the groundwork for

cooperation and the formation of a common brief and vision in other projects too. This provides the framework within which the different disciplines can cross-pollinate. And that leads in turn to intriguing projects for Rotterdam.

This text is based on conversations with Maurits Bongers, Rob van Schijndel, Maud Roukens, Rob Groeneweg and Martin Aarts. Their openness contributed significantly to the content of this article.

ALTERNATIVE FORMS OF MOBILITY

BIKE TAXI

PARK SHUTTLE

TAPIS ROULANT

Frans Botma

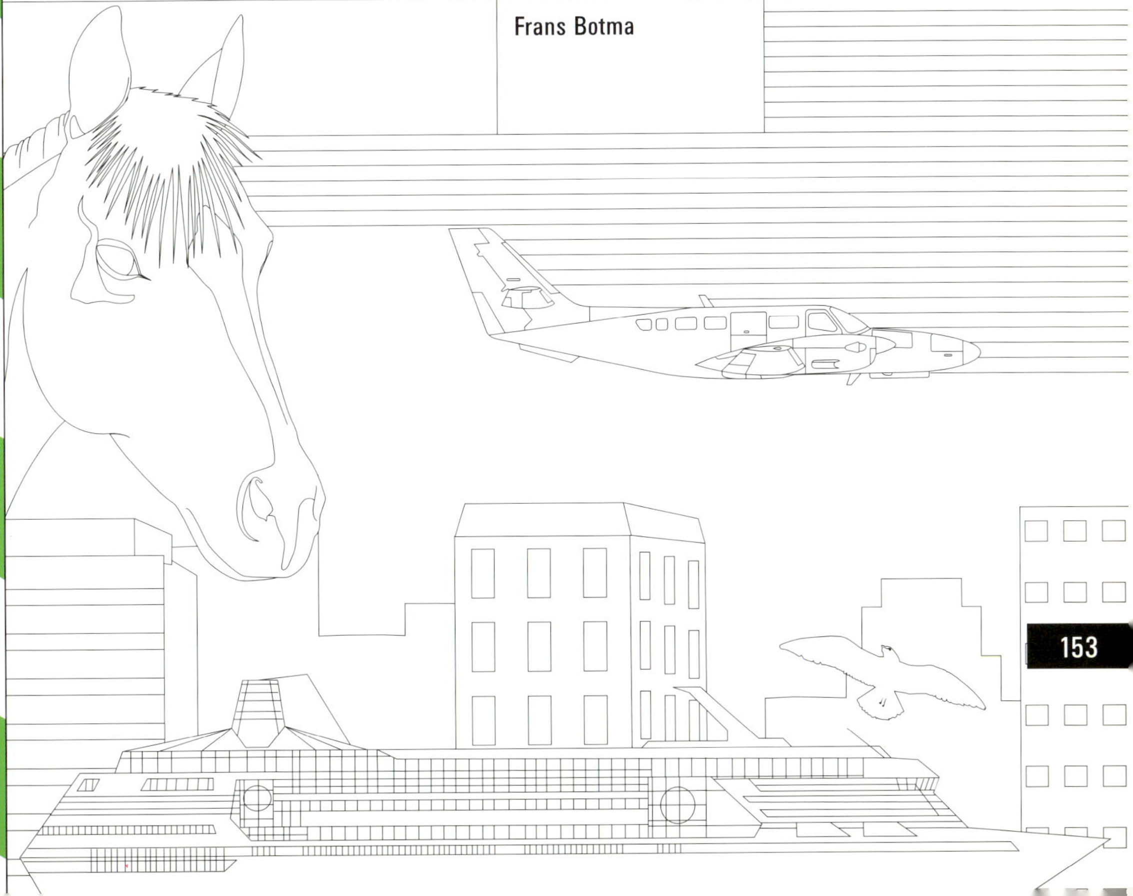

Rivium Park Shuttle

Year	1999
Initiator	Connexxion, Frog navigation systems
Speed	32 km/hour
Cost	2 strips (0.82 euro)
Where	Route between Kralingsezoom interchange and Rivium business park
Special features	Unmanned, automatic vehicle ('people-mover'). Due to the high demand a new vehicle is being developed to carry more passengers and there are plans to extend the route by an extra kilometre.
Contact	www.frog.nl

Bike Taxi

Year	1997
Idea	Berend Dekkers
Speed	0-10 km/hour
Cost	1 trip for 5 euro or 1 hour for 25 euro
Where	City centre during summer months and at festival sites
Special features	Environmentally friendly and surprisingly rapid mode of transport in the city centre.
Contact	www.starrotterdam.nl

Maas Taxi

Year	2001
Initiator	Daan van der Have and Hans Loos (Hotel New York)
Speed	60 km/hour
Cost	Initial tariff is 2.20 euro, then 1.65 euro per minute
Where	30 landing stages in Rotterdam
Special features	The quickest way to reach destinations along the Maas. Shipyard and boatmans' café of the Water Taxi at Hotel New York.
Contact	www.watertaxirotterdam.nl

Helicopter

Year	1907
Inventor	Paul Cornu
Speed	250 km/hour
Price	400 euro /hour
Where	Zestienhoven Airport, police, hospital
Special features	Exclusive mode of transport used by emergency services, corporations and private individuals because of its great flexibility and the avoidance of traffic congestion.
Contact	www.helikoptervluchten.nl www.traumahelikopter.nl

Water Taxi

Year	1993
Idea	Daan van der Have and Hans Loos
Speed	60 km/hour
Cost	2.30 euro from the Veerhaven and 3.00 euro from the Leuvehaven
Where	From Leuvehaven and Veerhaven to Hotel New York and back
Special features	For guests of Hotel New York.
Contact	www.watertaxirotterdam.nl

Skates

Year	1980
Idea	Scott and Brennan, ice-hockey players, United States
Speed	10-20 km/hour
Cost	Retail price: 50-250 euro
Where	Throughout the city on smooth asphalt, especially at the Blaak Skatepark, along the Maasboulevard, and in the Kralingse Bos and Bergse Bos recreation areas
Special features	Originally a niche modality, skating has grown into a popular form of mobility. The weekly Wednesday-night skate has grown into a veritable spectacle with thousands of enthusiastic skaters.
Contact	www.wednesdaynightskate.nl

Fast Ferry

Year	1999
An initiative of	Province of South Holland and Heijnen Doeksen shipping company
Speed	55 km/hour
Cost	Rotterdam-Dordrecht return: 5.75 euro
Where	Landing stages in Rotterdam, Ridderkerk and Alblasserdam
Special features	Bikes are transported for free, especially liked by day-trippers during the weekend.
Contact	www.fastferry.nl

Horse

Origin	Eurasia
Speed	0-40 km/hour
Where	There are eight riding schools in the City of Rotterdam
Special features	Bridleways in the Kralingse Bos and Bergse Bos recreation areas.
Contact	www.jockeyclub.nl www.vvv.rotterdam.nl

Greenwheels

Year	1995
Idea	Gijs van Lookeren Campagne and Jan Borghuis
Speed	0-120 km/hour
User's costs	5 euro per month + 5 euro per hour + 0.10 euro per kilometre
Where to find it	57 parking spots in Rotterdam, present in many other Dutch cities
Special features	Car-sharing system. There are specific parking places throughout the city, so a Greenwheels vehicle is always within walking distance of home. 'Your own car for now and then' – a concept for reserving a car by phone or via Internet.
Contact	www.greenwheels.nl

Tapis roulant for Pernis route cyclists to cross the Betuwe Line railway

Year	2002
Initiator	Rotterdam Municipal Port Management
Speed	3 km/hour
Cost	Free
Where	The crossing-point of Pernis cycle route and the Betuwe Line railway
Special features	Constructed for the crossing with the Betuwe Line railway.
Contact	www.hoogvliet.org

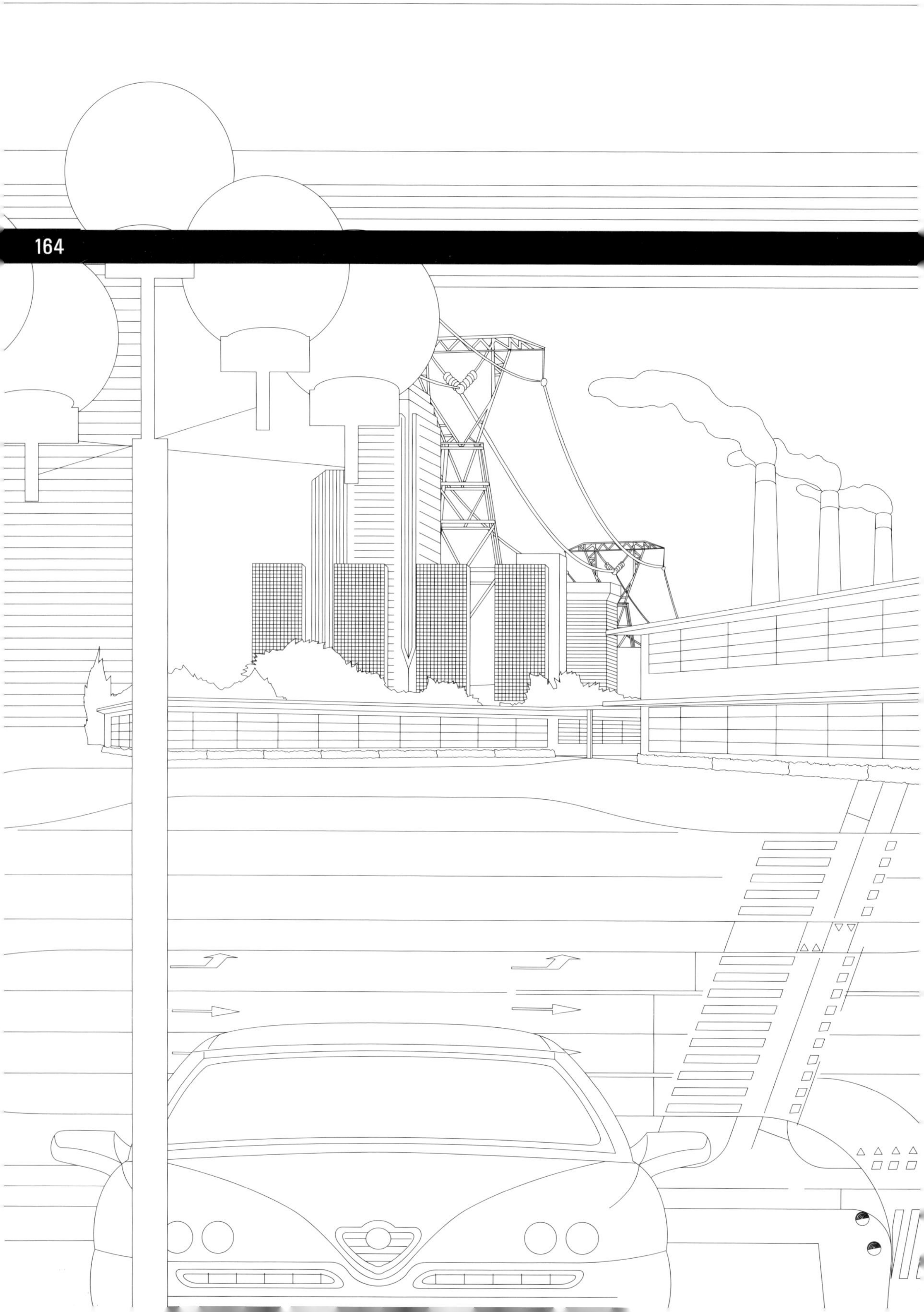

INTERDISCIPLINARY DESIGN

Marc Verheijen

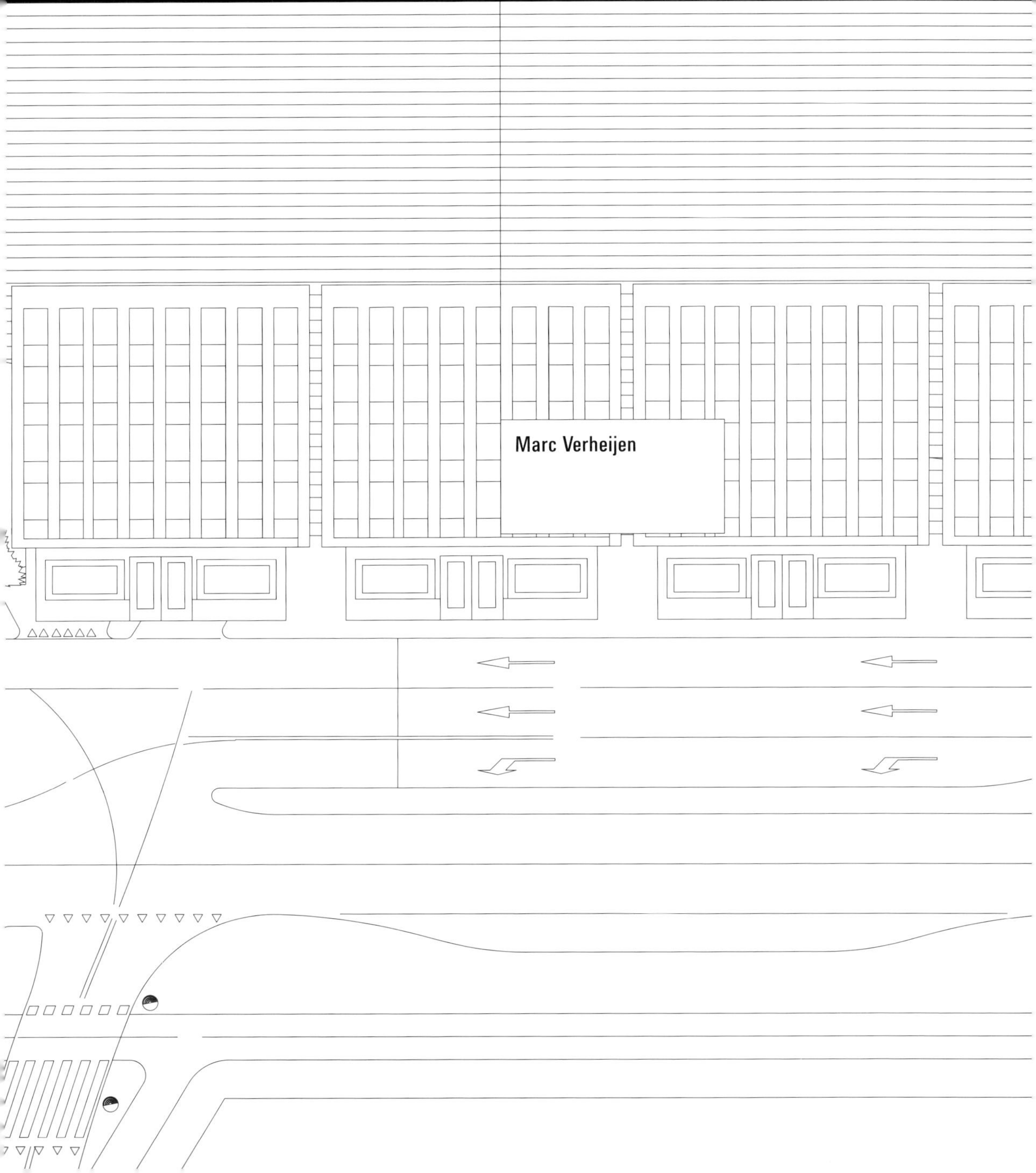

Mobility is about the dynamics of motion, movement and acceleration. At the same time mobility has to do with the physical facilities it requires, the infrastructure. Infrastructure is an outstanding example of a condition that facilitates social phenomena, making interaction between people possible. There is no such thing as a city without infrastructure. In its relation to a constantly developing and changing society the available infrastructure is by definition dated. Social developments always proceed faster than functions are changed or links are added to this extensive network. Societal pressure prompts maximum utilization of the network – double-decker instead of single-decker trains, night distribution, hard shoulders used as traffic lanes during rush hours, standing room instead of seats in regional trains, staggered holidays. These are all creative and effective solutions for maximum utilization of the available infrastructure for the societal mobility. However, there is little flexibility left in the existing system. Numerous innovations to improve the existing infrastructure are still conceivable, but they seem inadequate to meet the increase in mobility entailed by population growth and changes in activity and mobility patterns.
We are faced with a fundamental choice: restriction of individual and collective mobility or further expansion of the infrastructure network. Even restricting mobility involves a complex and extensive infrastructure challenge, if only to keep the network up-to-date. This challenge is primarily functional, such as solving network bottlenecks, increasing flow capacity, improving a pedestrian crossing or adding a new link to a cycle network. This one-dimensional approach detracts from the social significance of infrastructure. A purely functional approach to infrastructure leads to an undesirable segregation of mobility and city culture. Consider the acoustic barriers on motorways: they are indispensable to achieve an acceptable noise level for the surrounding houses, but they do nothing to stop exhaust fumes. A 'Berlin Wall' hundreds of kilometres long is rising inexorably; it already partitions the countryside. The acoustic barriers illustrate how infrastructure has been disconnected from society – infrastructure becoming functionally autonomous. In the long run, a growing society cannot afford such disconnection.

A new city bridge

Rotterdam is situated on both banks of the river Maas, a river approximately four hundred metres wide. There are seven permanent river crossings: a tunnel for cars, the metro, cyclists and pedestrians; a motorway bridge with a cycle lane; a railway tunnel; a metro tunnel; a tunnel for cars, cyclists and pedestrians and two city bridges. Exploratory studies for a possible new river crossing in the eastern section of the city are now being carried out, ranging from a ferry to a bridge. In this project the strategic significance of infrastructure can be illustrated with five different concepts for a new bridge. They differ only in respect of traffic type: an eco-bridge, a cycle bridge, a tram bridge, a car bridge and a combined bridge. These relatively small differences in traffic type provide a wide range of urban development potential.

Current situation

The locations on either bank being considered for the new bridge abutments have a peripheral character, despite their central situation in the urban area. The north bank consists of a rural dike, the edge of a residential area of average density, a business park mostly for car dealers, a military barracks, a cemetery and various sports fields and garden allotments. Some distance away there are office areas and the university campus. The south bank consists of the outskirts of a pre-war residential district, large-scale railway and road infrastructure, the stadium, retail businesses and the Kop van Zuid, in full development. In programme, demography, functions and space they are two highly contrasting worlds.

Eco-bridge

A new river crossing designed specifically for flora and fauna, creating a strip of green between the two banks, which the city dweller can only use as a walking route. An eco-bridge will bring the open and natural area, 'polder de Esch', on the north bank in direct relation with the densely built and intensively used districts on the south bank. It promises the city dweller a unique promenade.

An eco-bridge will also be a link between park zones and greenbelt structures of greater magnitude. The habitat of organisms living in urban areas will be expanded. The eastern section of the city will acquire an extensive greenbelt – from the river Rotte area through Kralingsebos, polder de Esch and the eco-bridge to the Zuiderpark. The eco-bridge will have an enormous impact on nature development and recreation. It would also have worldwide significance in the field of urban culture: a city constructing a 400-metre bridge for plants, walkers and skaters! However, the eco-bridge has hardly any relevance for urban mobility.

Cycle bridge

A new river crossing designed specifically for cyclists, adding a link to the urban and regional cycle network on both banks. A cycle bridge will provide an interesting mobility link. It will make the use of bicycles in the eastern section of the city more direct and faster than the use of public transport or cars. A bicycle is cheap to buy and to use, and cycling is also healthy and environmentally friendly.

The cycle bridge, for instance, will make it more attractive for students at the Erasmus University (north bank) to look for accommodation in the southern residential districts, where there is a large supply of relatively cheap housing. For various districts on the south bank the presence of students might mean diversification of the population and the development of new facilities. Besides, the cycle bridge forms an interesting link in the recreational cycle network on a regional scale and connects the southern islands with the Rotte area and the Groene Hart ('Green Heart') rural area in the central Netherlands.

For safety reasons it is by no means certain that a cycle bridge would be used much at night.

Tram bridge

A new river crossing designed specifically for trams, adding an important link will be added to the tram network on both banks. The bridge will make an east tangent feasible, and junctions outside the city centre can be directly connected with each other. Thus a tram connection from Zuidplein through Kralingsezoom and Parkstad to Alexander will be possible, with a direct link to the railway network. Forecasts indicate significant 'transport tension' on this section, so many people will be using it, a portion of whom never made this trip before, but will when there is a direct tram connection. People now making this trip by car are also likely to choose the good alternative of the tram in the future. Consequently, a tram bridge will have a positive effect on the 'modal split' (the choice of means of transport) and will also lead to more exchange between the north and south banks. In addition to the students and recreational users mentioned in the example of the cycle bridge, these will also include commuters.

Car bridge

A new river crossing designed specifically for cars, adding a link to the urban and regional car network on both banks. This will result in a large-scale shift in flows of car traffic, which may have a nation-wide effect. The car network is so overloaded that any addition will be utilised immediately.
A comparison of car traffic with water is appropriate: where it can flow, it flows. If the car bridge is directly connected to the main infrastructure, part of the motorway traffic may even prefer a route through the city via the car bridge. A car bridge will give both banks extensive programmatic potential, notably for business, retail and entertainment programmes.

City bridge

A new river crossing designed for cars, trams, cyclists and pedestrians, adding a link to the mobility network on both banks on different scales. Building a city bridge seems to make use of all the above-mentioned advantages and possibilities. However, this is not the case. Some of the opportunities opened up by developing a bridge from the perspective of one modality clash with others. The qualities an eco-bridge makes possible are to a certain extent negated if a large flow of cars is added. A tram bridge and a cycle bridge can be combined easily without affecting their potentials. If cars are added, however, the network advantages of tram and bicycle as compared to the car no longer apply. For that reason a city bridge does not provide a 'sum total of advantages'. It will be more generic, it will possibly be executed to a lesser extreme, it will make all sorts of things possible, but a maximization of accessibility will not be feasible. The city bridge will benefit from access points within the city, from both banks. The more or less peripheral character of both banks will have to be urbanised in order to make the most of a city bridge. In concrete terms this amounts to the construction of a boulevard with a separate tramline, cycle paths and broad pavements on which large urban blocks are situated, with plinth functions (shops and facilities) on the ground floor and housing and work on the floors above. The advantages for the tram and cycle network will than be combined with the 'address quality' of automobile access. As the route becomes more urban, the city bridge will lose its appeal as a short cut for motorway-related car traffic.

The five alternatives for a new river crossing illustrate the divergent urban impacts arising from a relatively limited infrastructure intervention. The example makes it clear that the consequences of an infrastructure intervention are not merely functional and related to traffic, or limited to the area directly covered by the plan. Such an intervention will also have an effect outside that area, and will make itself felt on a local, urban and even regional scale.

Five-dimensional

Infrastructure can have different meanings and dimensions. The example of the city bridge illustrates that it is questionable whether filling in the project, formulating the solution, making the design choices or taking the decisions should be predominantly based on functional grounds. As cities and urban agglomerations increase in density, their infrastructure can no longer be viewed as a purely functional and autonomous object, detached from its environment. Infrastructure is part of the urban context and should be brought into balance with this context. This is not limited to the physical, spatial sense, but is also aimed at the dynamic and tempographic significance of mobility. For instance, infrastructure frequently has an important programmatic dimension, a positive quality that can be exploited by looking for optimal links. New infrastructure creates new addresses, making new buildings possible. By definition an optimal merging of programme and infrastructure will be more mobility-friendly than the familiar industrial parks in the pastures. For that matter, these are only viable because of the extensive infrastructure that 'goes out there'.

Infrastructure has an enormous social dimension. It enables physical interaction between people and groups, exchange of ideas and thoughts, sharing of emotions. Where large flows come together there is friction, and friction creates warmth! The drawback of the social dimension of infrastructure is the risk of exclusion, inaccessibility, isolation. The most mobile human being in a western society, a vagrant, is at the same time usually the most socially isolated!

The infrastructure project also has a large spatial dimension. A century ago this was a logical element of the brief: in the designs of parkways and the first motorways in Europe a maximum experience of the landscape played an important part in the drawing of the route. After decades of neglect for the spatial dimension, there has been talk in recent years of landscaping roadways or concealing railway lines behind screens of green. However, this remains limited to mere window-dressing without addressing separation. Introduction, as the word indicates, means introducing something autonomous (an object, an independent entity) into the context (the surroundings, the other). Thus the one and the other continue to exist and so does spatial separation. The example of the parklanes is clearly reaches further – a new unity arises where road and surroundings together acquire a new meaning, relate to and reinforce each other.

At the moment very little attention is paid to the cultural dimension of mobility, which is nevertheless of great importance. Urban life is increasingly taking place in the transit spaces of the cities. Infrastructure greatly affects the identity of cities and the urban image. Los Angeles can hardly be dissociated from its motorways, New York and Barcelona from their grid structures, Venice and Amsterdam from their canals, Paris from its boulevards, London from the Underground, Rotterdam from the river Maas. Not every street has such an impact. But the comparison of a photograph of a residential street in the sixties with one of a residential street in a new housing estate definitely illustrates that they reflect the spirit of the times in which they were laid out. Thus a street is an expression of an element of culture: designing infrastructure is designing culture.

The often functional origin of an infrastructure brief therefore has five dimensions: functional, programmatic, social, spatial and cultural. Consequently, it is necessary to design infrastructure in five dimensions in order to do justice to its social impact and urban significance. In that way mobility can contribute to urban culture and urban development in a responsible manner.

Strategic power

Infrastructure is one of the means by which urban culture and urban development can be influenced. The development of infrastructure, working on the extensive and complex network, has an enormous strategic power. With a simple intervention new urban potential can be tapped. Likewise a whole neighbourhood can be isolated by closing off a street or closing down a tram stop. Infrastructure can create conditions to initiate and direct social developments. If this is done well, infrastructure has the power to regulate and 'make possible', with an equal potential to deregulate and destroy when things go wrong. Because of this strategic power, infrastructure has a great impact on urban development and consequently decisions on infrastructure have a great impact on urban culture.

Frequently, however, this strategic power cannot be put to optimal use. This makes sense, since infrastructure is not intended for an individual and is usually not limited to a simple, cheap and small-scale intervention.

The complexity of infrastructure often turns infrastructure planning and development into a cumbersome and slow process. Infrastructure is extremely expensive. The high-speed railway line (HSL) from the Belgian border to Amsterdam, approximately 100 kilometres long, will cost 5.3 billion euro. A simple calculation shows that this means 53 million euro per kilometre or 53,000 euro per metre. The HSL passes various boundaries: national borders, provincial borders, municipal boundaries, water board districts, private property, ecological boundaries, and so on. A great number of parties are directly involved, consisting of a small group of professionals who wish to build the railway line out of societal considerations and a large group of people who will be negatively affected by the railway line, who may even have to abandon their houses or birthplace for a train which they themselves will perhaps never use. These are some aspects making an infrastructure project a laborious and complicated affair. Nor, in the main, are the burdens of a project 'earned back' within the project boundaries and within the amortization period. The benefit of an infrastructure project is often less direct and less measurable and can definitely not be assessed merely from

a functional or financial perspective. Here too, the five previously mentioned dimensions play a part. The intervention should produce societal benefits and should therefore, aside from being functional, also have significance in the programmatic, social, spatial and cultural dimensions. This can be a specific aim right from the initial formulation of the brief.

The example of the 'new city bridge' illustrates this strategic power. Numerous examples from the past can also be cited. The construction of the Nieuwe Waterweg positioned Rotterdam directly on the sea and thus made possible the growth of the Port of Rotterdam. The programmatic and cultural impact of that intervention was enormous. The channel tunnel has made the exchange between the Continent and England simpler, faster and cheaper. Although this was specifically devised from a functional perspective, during the planning process the debate in England centred primarily on the cultural impact of the intervention: will England still be England when there is a permanent Channel crossing? The extensive European motorway network has brought regions closer together and given the urban peripheries greater significance. Now the motorways are the major identity bearers of a city and have a great spatial and cultural impact. The Dutch know Lyon as that dirty town where there are so many traffic jams during the summer holidays. The perception of a rail traveller getting off in the centre of Lyon is quite different: a clean, luxurious, historical city centre with beautiful pedestrian squares with water features. That is why a station on the European high-speed railway network is so important for cities. Obviously this is functional (a fast, comfortable and safe journey), but also specifically programmatic, spatial and cultural. The social impact of high-speed trains is large but hard to measure.

Interdisciplinary

On the basis of design research or rather exploratory design, the various dimensions of infrastructure can be defined and assessed. This is extremely complex. However, it is vital that choices involving infrastructure be based on such profound and exhaustive research. Development of the infrastructure network cannot be limited to one single discipline. Traffic engineers are indispensable in these projects, although these are questions *par excellence* spanning the full spatial planning spectrum. Every discipline within this spectrum can make a significant contribution. This book is a call for interdisciplinary design – using sector-based know-how and skills from various disciplines to contribute to interdisciplinary design research. This approach to the infrastructure brief is not only a matter of design. Exploring and developing city, urbanity, culture and infrastructure in this way also sets requirements for the formulation of the brief and the decision-making process. Interdisciplinary design can succeed only if the organisational, financial, procedural and administrative conditions allow for it.

ROTTERDAM

STERKER DOOR STRIJD

Mobility can be represented in histograms, diagrams and statistics. This data makes the elusive phenomenon of the city – in this case Rotterdam – more easy to manage.

Harko Stolte

S ROTTERDAM CITY

S ROTTERDAM CITY CENTRE

R ROTTERDAM DISTRICT

H ROTTERDAM HARBOUR

2001 AANTAL INWONERS

S

2000 AANTAL INWONERS

592.673	632.366	546.968	546.419	450.000	444.987
ROTTERDAM	GENUA	BREMEN	NANTES	EDINBURG	ANTWERPEN

2001 AANTAL INWONERS

R

1.175.952

AANTAL ARBEIDSPLAATSEN

S

1993	1994	1995	1996	1997	1998	1999
274.200	266.600	260.400	259.300	269.100	284.000	294.800

2001 LENGTE NETWERK

1.750 KM | 50 KM

GEMIDDELDE SNELHEID [BINNENSTAD]

	SPITS	BUITEN-SPITS
ROTTERDAM	20	30
GENUA	18	30
HELSINKI	22	26
MILAN	18	25
EDINBURG	13	
BARCELONA	30	55

2001 AUTOBEZIT

ROTTERDAM	AMSTERDAM	DEN HAAG	UTRECHT	NEDERLAND
188.374	234.025	145.187	103.787	6.539.212

AUTOBEZIT PER 1.000 INWONERS

	ROTTERDAM	AMSTERDAM	DEN HAAG	UTRECHT	NEDERLAND
1997	298	294	317	359	369
2001	316	319	328	405	409

2001 AUTOBEZIT PER 1.000 INWONERS

ROTTERDAM	GENUA	BREMEN	NANTES	EDINBURG	ANTWERPEN
316	482	459	475	283	433

2002 BRANDSTOF PRIJZEN

	DIESEL	EUROLOODVRIJ
NL	0.78	1.15
L	0.63	0.77
ES	0.68	0.81
CH	0.92	0.93
B	0.75	1.02
AU	0.80	0.95
F	0.76	1.00
D	0.81	1.03
I	0.85	1.12
GB	1.15	1.18

BRANDSTOFGEBRUIK IN kTon PER JAAR

		BENZINE	DIESEL	LPG
1990	NL	3.5	3.7	0.9
1999	NL	4.1	5.1	0.6

2002 AANTAL AUTO'S PER DAG

STEDELIJKE ROUTE
MAASTUNNEL

59.179

BINNENSTADSWEG
WEENA

20.113

WEG NAAR KANTOORGEBIED
BRAINPARK

2.560

2002 UURVERDELING AUTOVERKEER

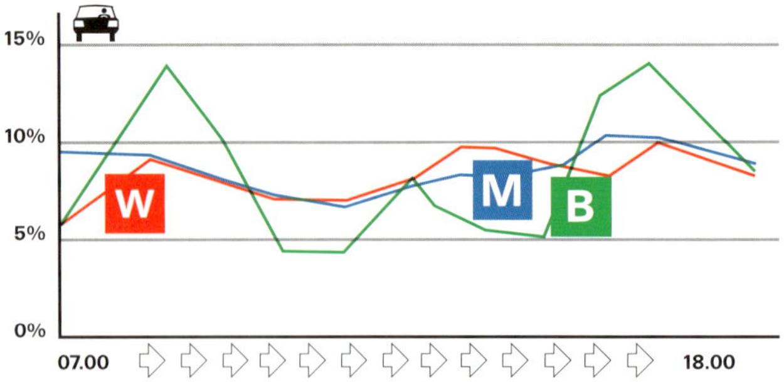

GROEI AUTOVERKEER 07.00 – 19.00 UUR

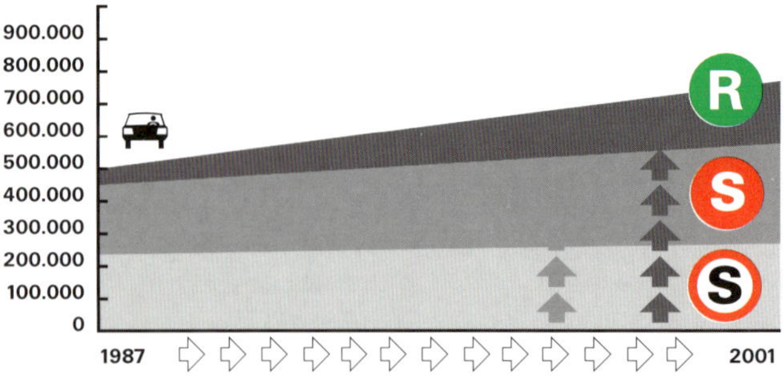

2002 GEMIDDELDE SNELHEID INVALSROUTES

	MAX. SNELHEID	SPITS
PARKLANE	50	30
STADHOUDERSWEG	50	30
SCHIEKADE	50	15
MAASBOULEVARD	50	36
STADIONWEG	50	27
VAANWEG	50	18
DORPSWEG	50	28

VAANWEG > MAASTUNNEL

TIJD	REISTIJD	TIJD	REISTIJD	TIJD	REISTIJD
01.00	7 MINUTEN	09.00	11 MINUTEN	17.00	7 MINUTEN
02.00	7 MINUTEN	10.00	9 MINUTEN	18.00	8 MINUTEN
03.00	7 MINUTEN	11.00	7 MINUTEN	19.00	8 MINUTEN
04.00	7 MINUTEN	12.00	7 MINUTEN	20.00	7 MINUTEN
05.00	7 MINUTEN	13.00	7 MINUTEN	21.00	6 MINUTEN
06.00	7 MINUTEN	14.00	7 MINUTEN	22.00	6 MINUTEN
07.00	8 MINUTEN	15.00	7 MINUTEN	23.00	6 MINUTEN
08.00	11 MINUTEN	16.00	8 MINUTEN	24.00	7 MINUTEN

2001 AANTAL PARKEERPLAATSEN S

6.589 | 3.021 | 10.422 | 11.185 | 2.766 | 685

2003 UURTARIEF S

1.85 EURO PER UUR

ROTTERDAM

2001 UURTARIEF

Stad	Tarief
ROTTERDAM	1.60 EURO PER UUR
BREMEN	1.00 EURO PER UUR
NANTES	1.00 EURO PER UUR
EDINBURG	2.30 EURO PER UUR
DRESDEN	1.13 EURO PER UUR
GENUA	1.55 EURO PER UUR

2002 BEZETTING PARKEERGARAGES OP ZONDAG S

OPEN 12.00 – 23.00

	IN	UIT	BEZETTING
11.00 – 12.00	0	41	681
12.00 – 13.00	1.200	208	1.365
13.00 – 14.00	1.037	549	2.212
14.00 – 15.00	954	774	2.634
15.00 – 16.00	796	953	2.722
16.00 – 17.00	380	1.127	2.461
17.00 – 18.00	262	1.006	1.547
18.00 – 19.00	293	380	1.010
19.00 – 20.00	343	182	1.037
20.00 – 21.00	211	224	1.156
21.00 – 22.00	146	255	1.142
22.00 – 23.00	108	304	1.026

2000 AANTAL PLAATSEN PER 1.000 INWONERS

P+R	Aantal
ROTTERDAM	4.6
BREMEN	2.5
EDINBURG	0.6
MILAAN	5.3
HELSINKI	4.7

2001 LENGTE NETWERK FIETSPADEN

2000 LENGTE NETWERK PER 1.000 INWONERS

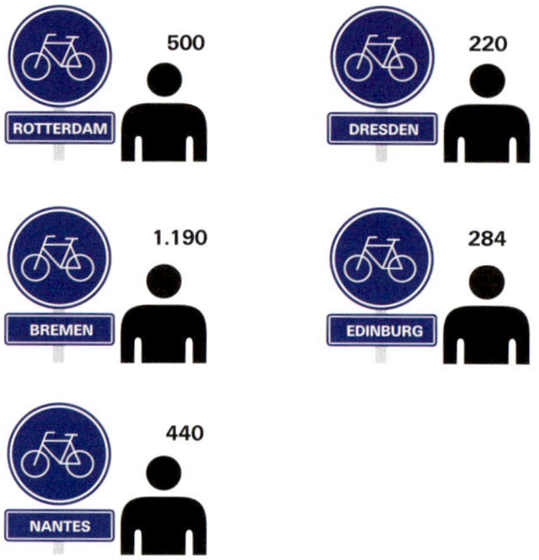

2001 FIETSVERPLAATSINGEN ALS DEEL VAN TOTALE AANTAL VERPLAATSINGEN

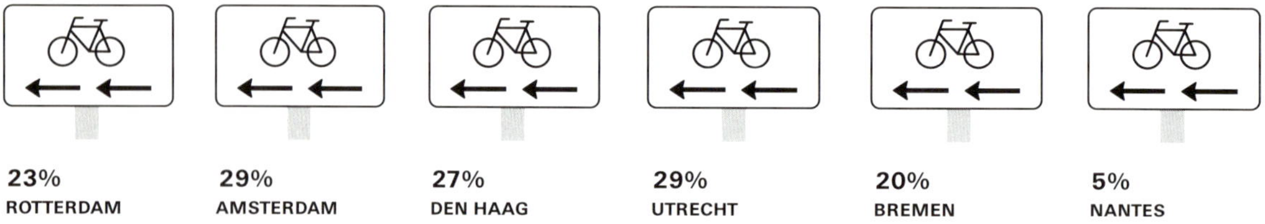

AANTAL [BROM]FIETSERS VAN EN NAAR DE BINNENSTAD

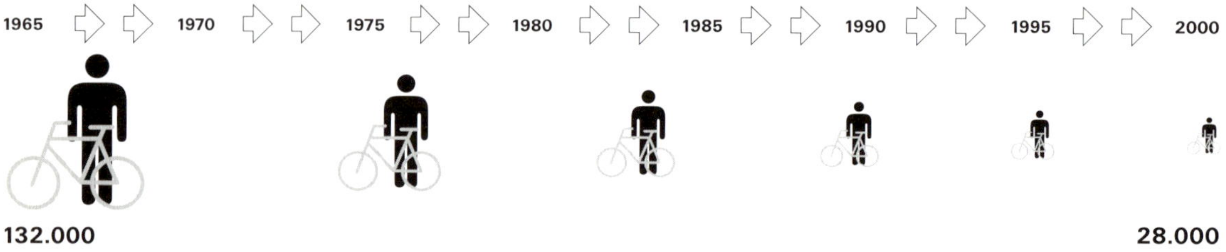

AANTAL [BROM]FIETSERS OVER DE MAAS

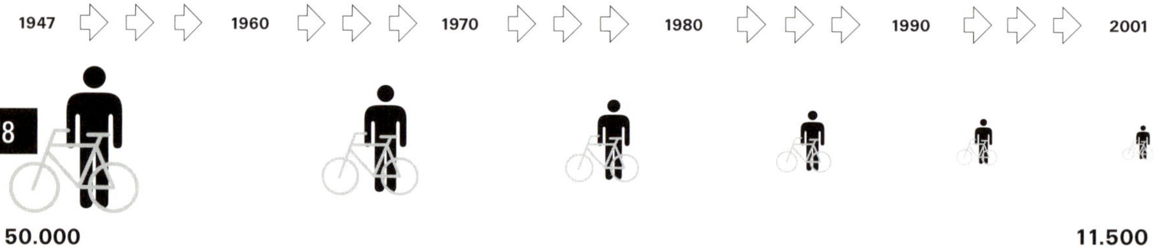

2001 DAGVERLOOP FIETSGEBRUIK S

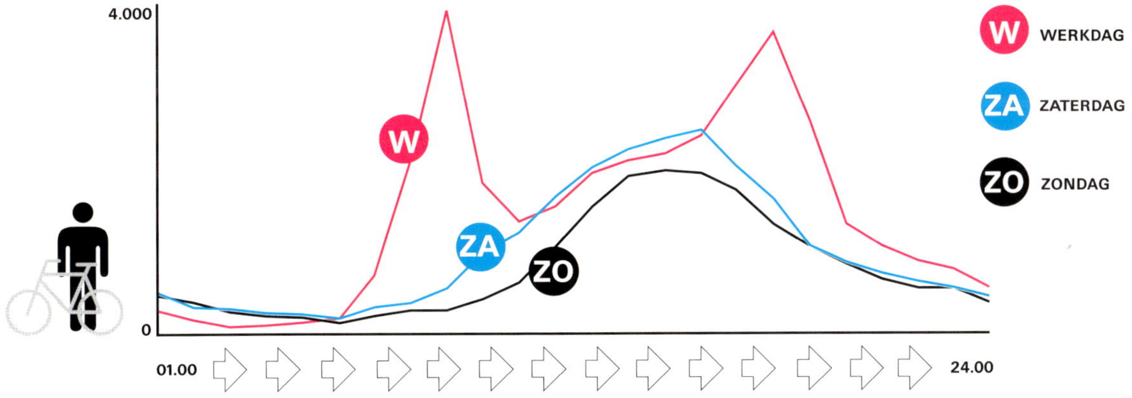

2001 AUTOMOBILISTEN OVER FIETSEN

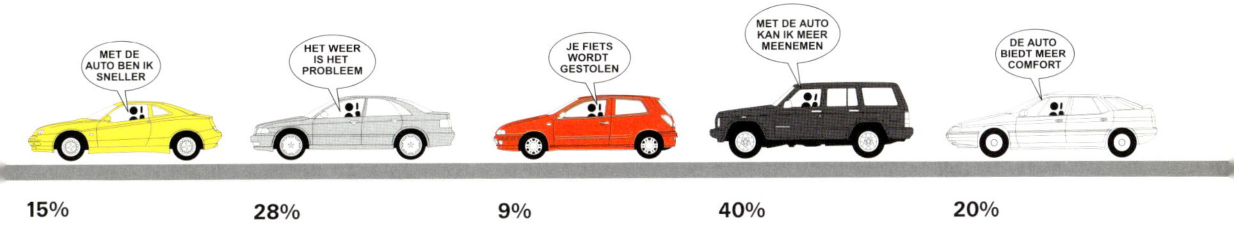

2001 OV PASSAGIERS OVER FIETSEN

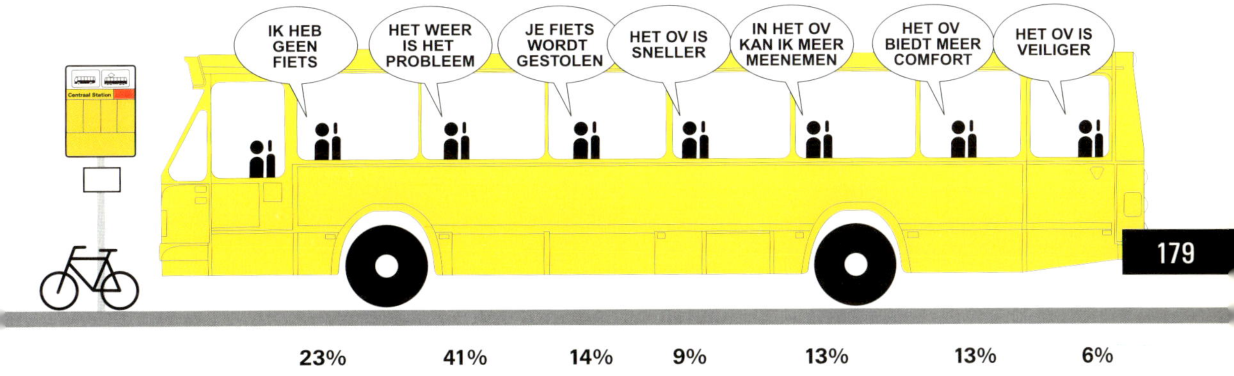

2001 LENGTE NETWERK

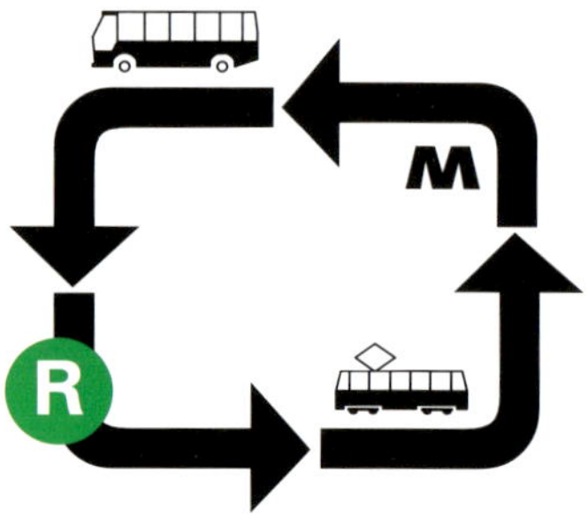

1.112 KM

2001 AANTAL HALTES

1.008

2001 LENGTE NETWERK [PER KM²]

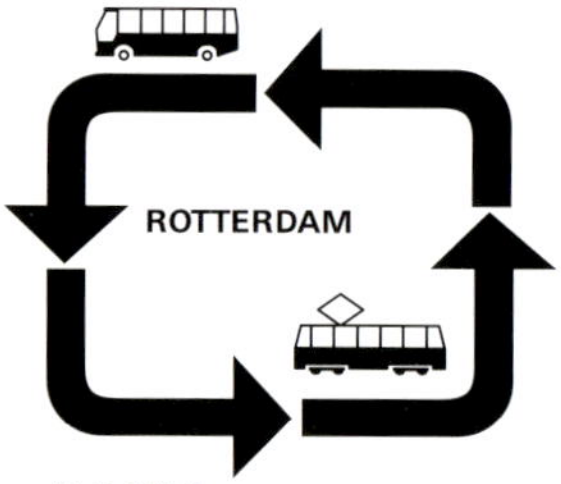

2.6 KM

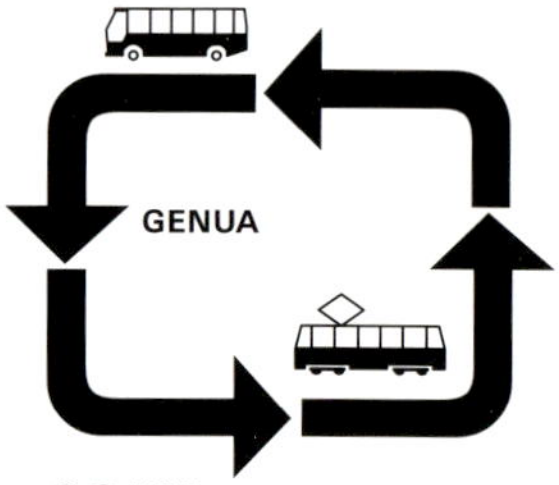

3.8 KM

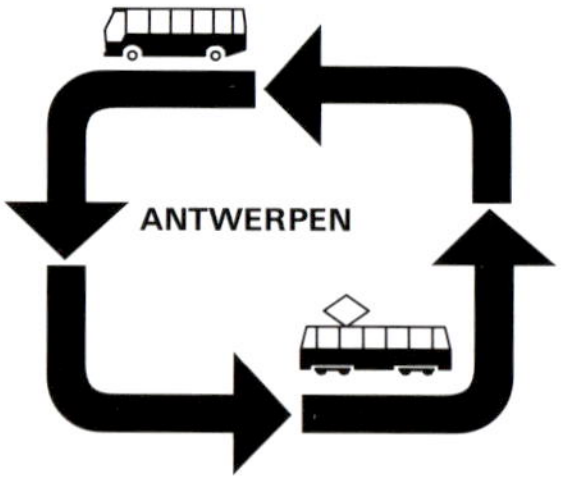

3.4 KM

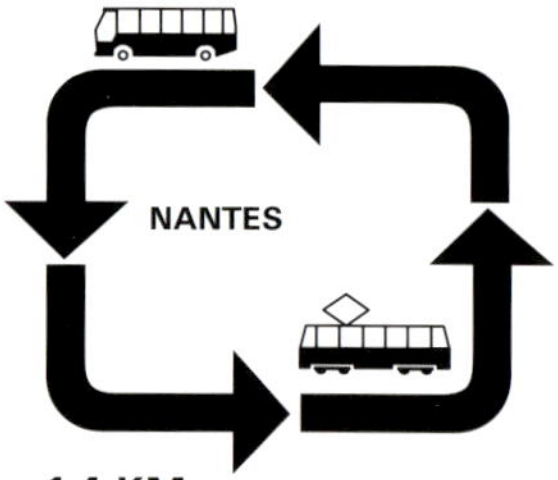

1.4 KM

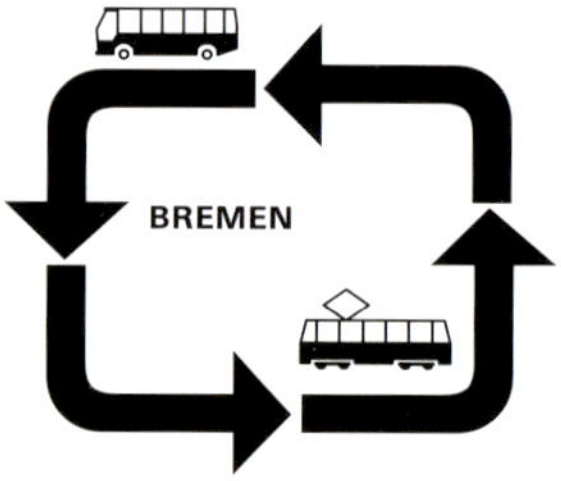

1.7 KM

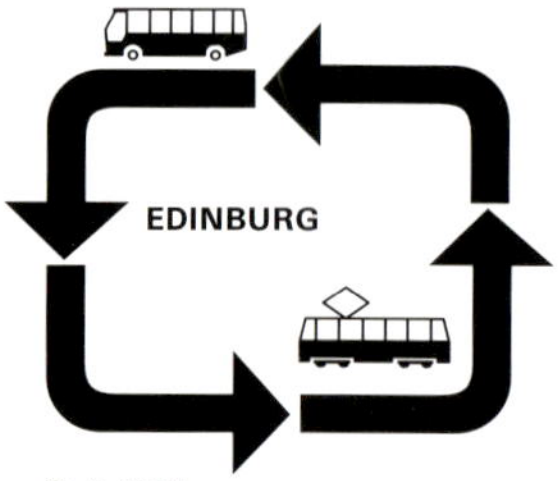

3.4 KM

2001 HALTES PER KM²

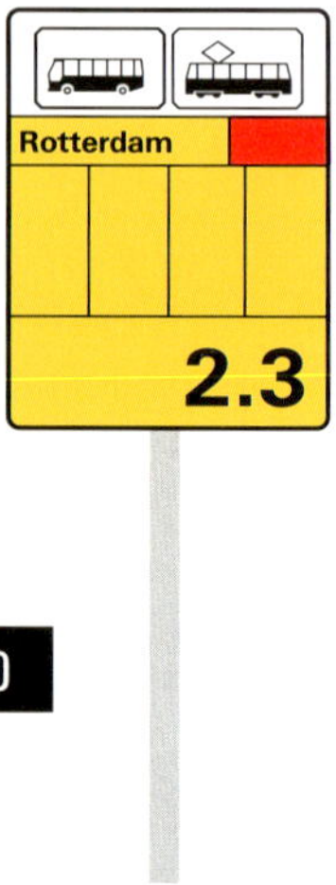

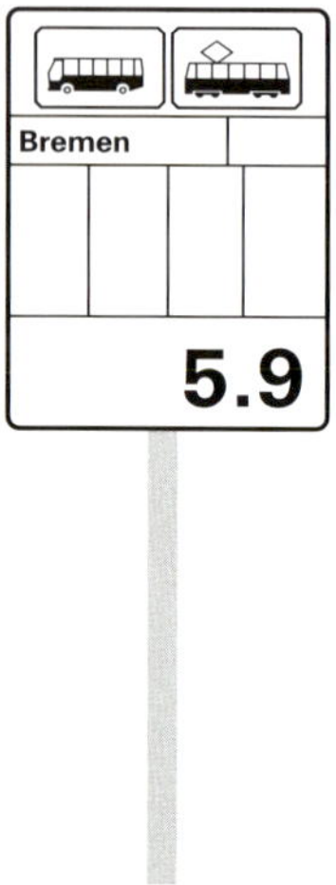

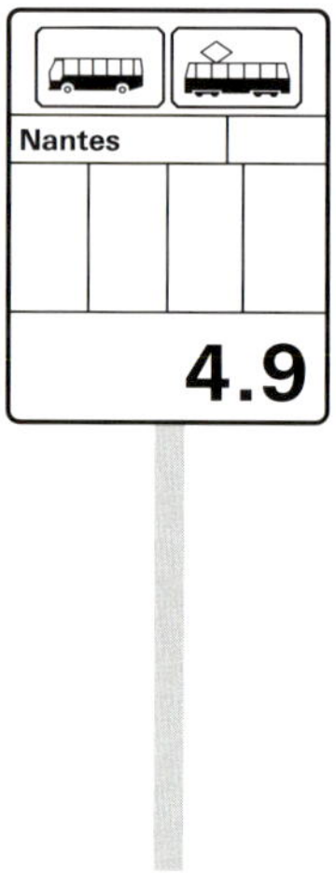

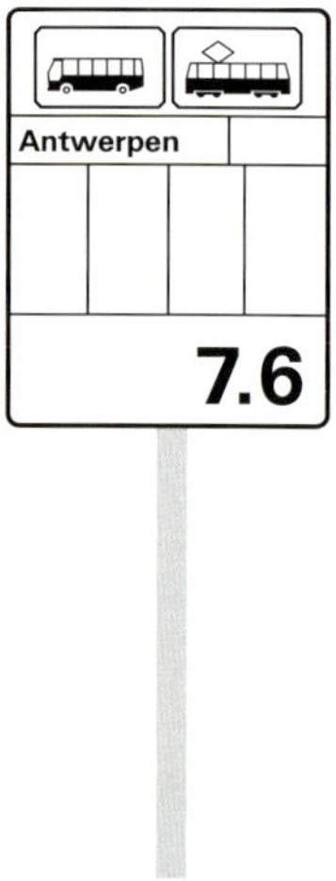

2001 OPENBAAR VERVOER REIZIGERS PER HALTE PER DAG

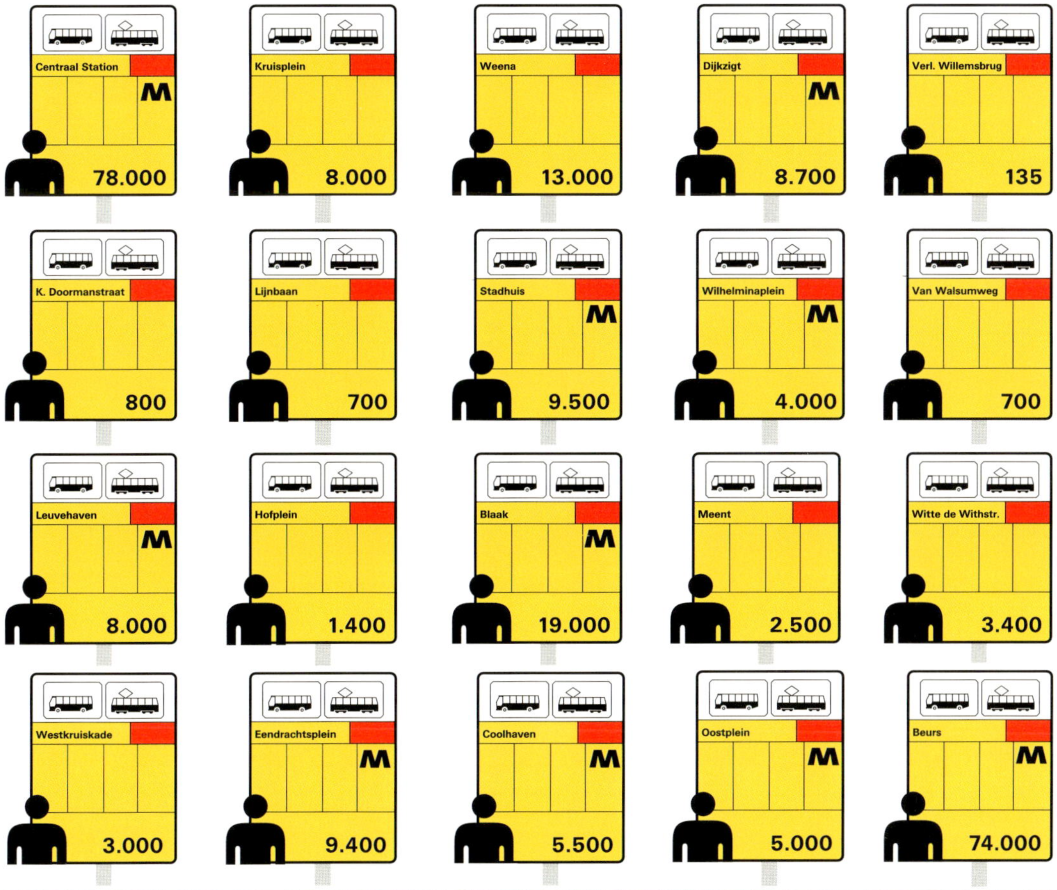

1999 AANTAL HALTES STATION ZUIDPEIN

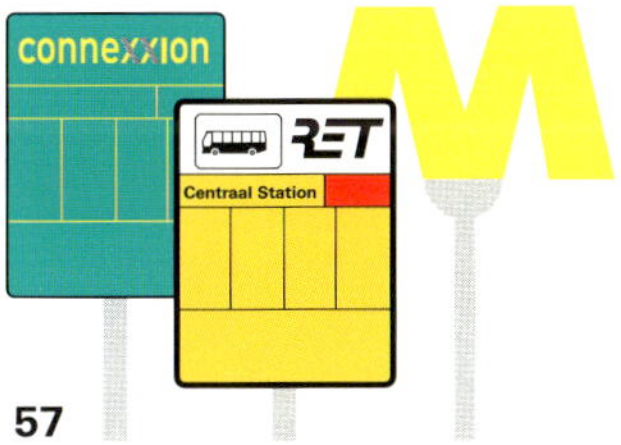

1999 AANTAL REIZIGERS PER DAG STATION ZUIDPEIN

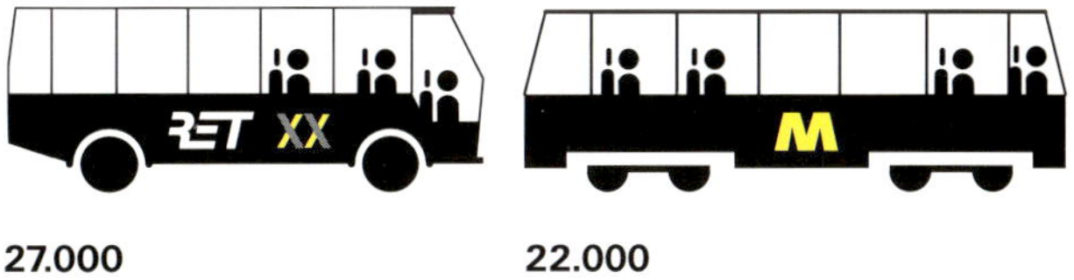

1999 AANTAL OVERSTAPPEN PER DAG STATION ZUIDPEIN

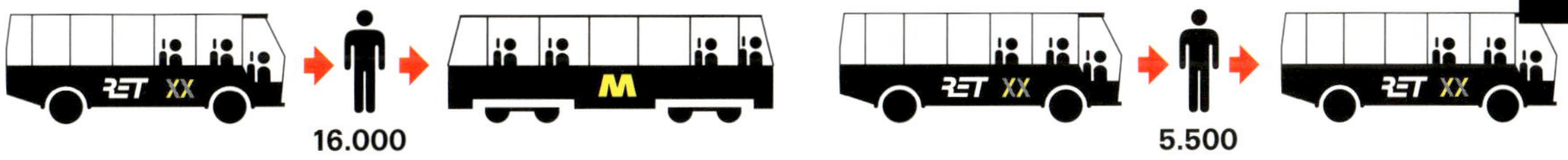

MODAL SPLIT

2001 VERVOER BINNEN DE STAD

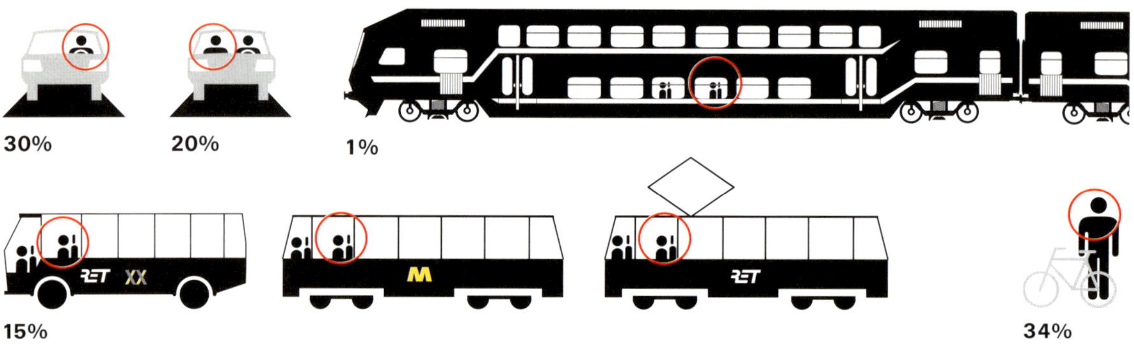

2001 VERVOER VAN EN NAAR DE STAD

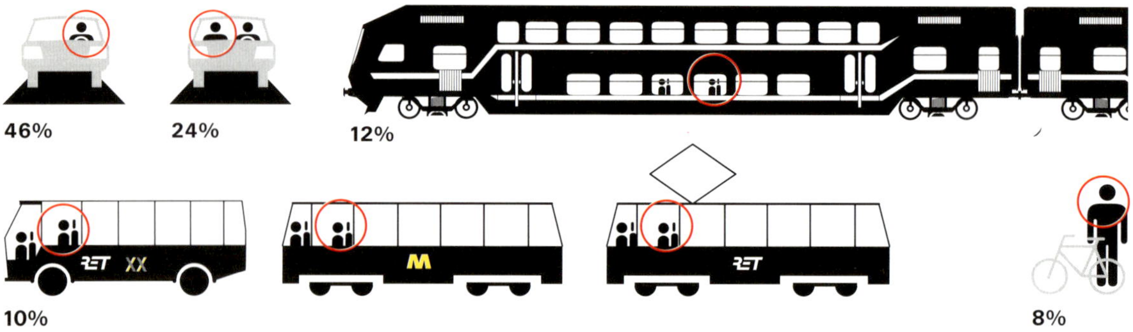

2002 VERDELING VERVOERSWIJZEN

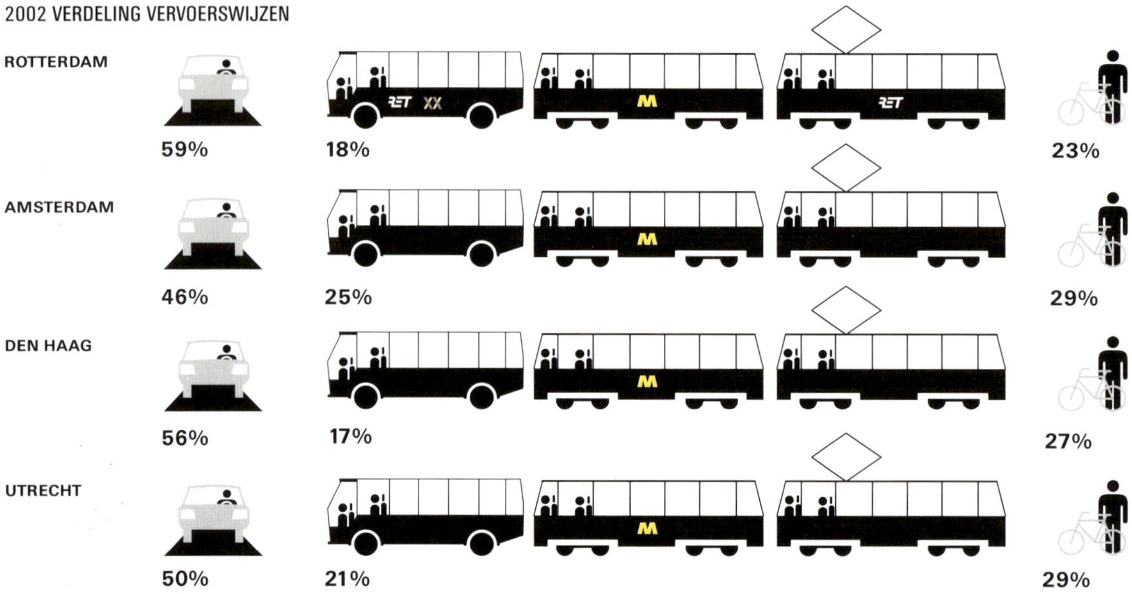

MODAL SPLIT

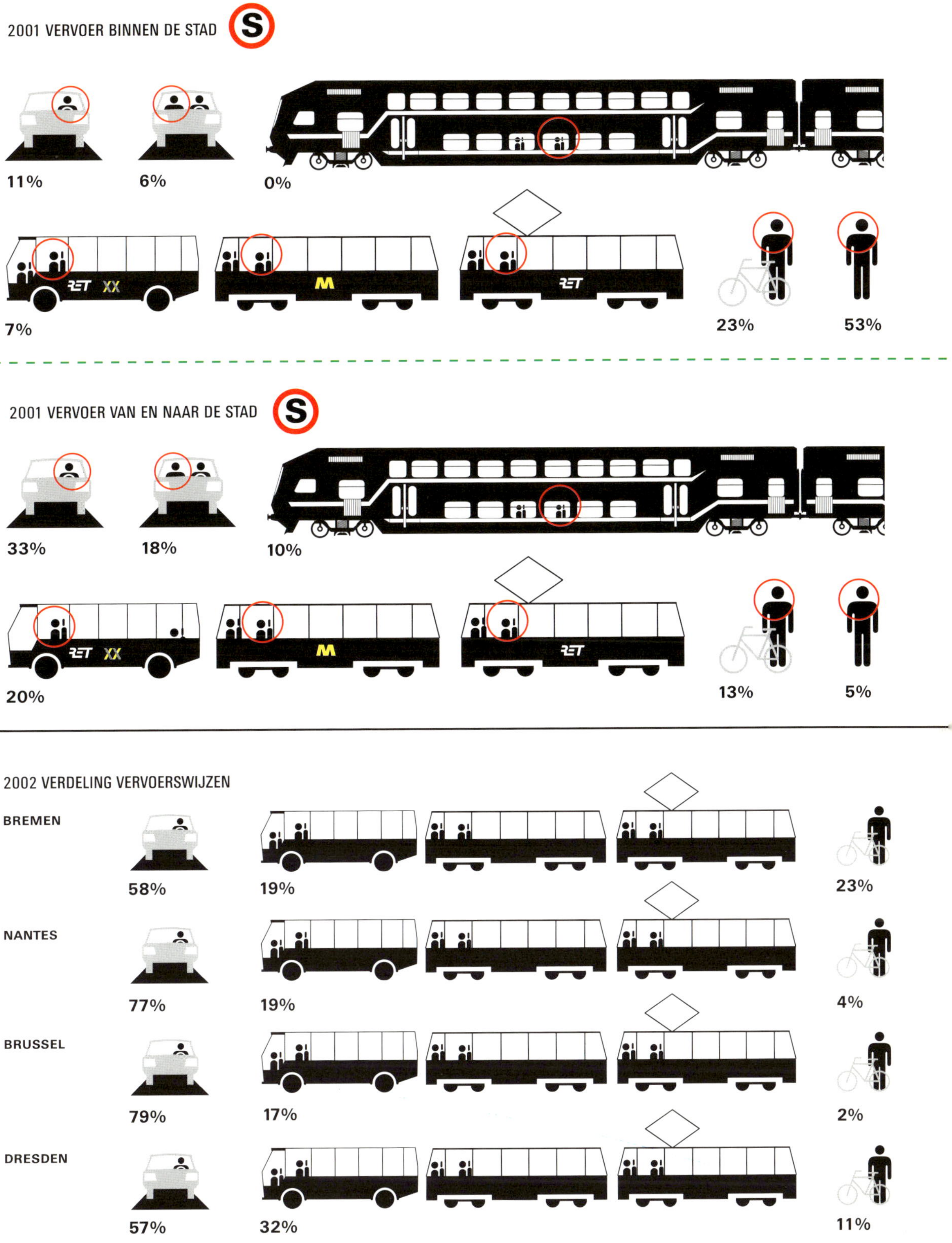
2001 VERVOER BINNEN DE STAD
S
11%
6%
0%
RET
XX
M
RET
7%
23%
53%
2001 VERVOER VAN EN NAAR DE STAD
S
33%
18%
10%
RET
XX
M
RET
20%
13%
5%
2002 VERDELING VERVOERSWIJZEN
BREMEN
58%
19%
23%
NANTES
77%
19%
4%
BRUSSEL
79%
17%
2%
DRESDEN
57%
32%
11%

2001 REIZIGERS PER DAG OP OEVERVERBINDING

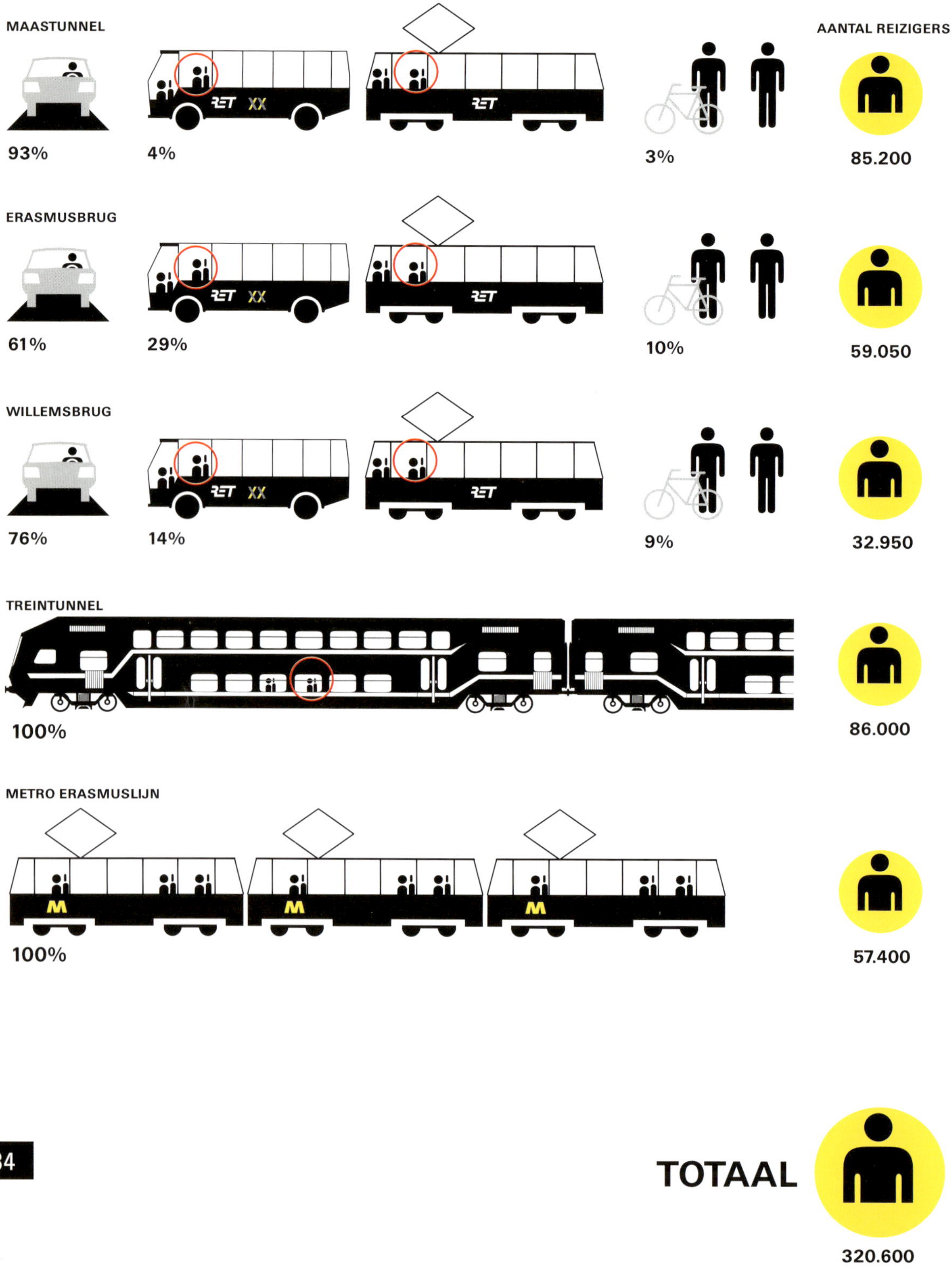

2000 AANTAL VERKEERSSLACHTOFFERS PER 1.000 INWONERS

ROTTERDAM	4 GROTE STEDEN	35 GROTE STEDEN	NEDERLAND
3.54	3.58	2.83	2.97

2000 VERDELING ONGEVALLEN OVER VERVOERSWIJZEN S

OVERIG

58%	10%	1%	31%

2000 VERDELING SLACHTOFFERS NAAR VERVOERSWIJZEN S

61%	17%	13%	9%

BLOOTSTELLING VERKEERSDEELNEMERS

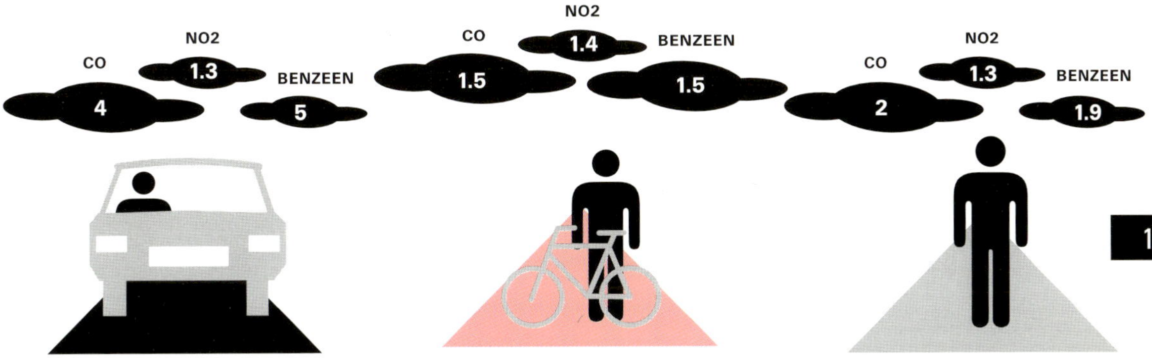

AANTAL INSTALLATIES

1974	1982	1990	2000	2003
137	166	208	245	237

AANTAL INSTALLATIES REAGEREND OP VERKEERSAANBOD

1974	1982	1990	2000	2003
10	45	145	245	237

2002 AANTAL LAMPEN

18.500

2002 VERVANGEN LAMPEN

615

1998 INSTALLATIES 'S NACHTS BUITEN WERKING

45%

2002 AANTAL VERKEERSBORDEN S H

4.833 1.288

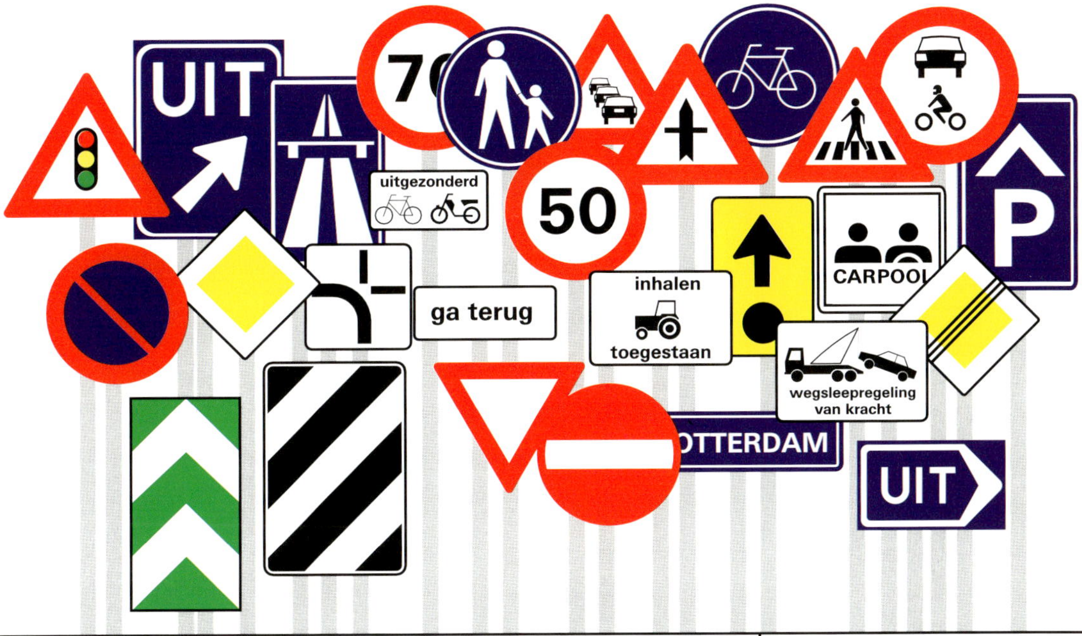

2002 AANTAL BRUGGEN R

38

2002 AANTAL SLUIZEN R

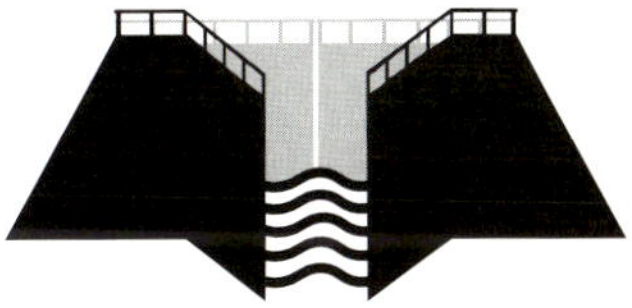

8

2002 AANTAL TUNNELS R

8

2000 CONTAINERS PER JAAR

6.275.000.000
ROTTERDAM

4.248.000.000
HAMBURG

4.082.000.000
ANTWERPEN

2.800.000.000
FELIXSTOWE

2.737.000.000
BREMEN

2001 OPPERVLAKTE HAVEN

W 3.500 HA

B 4.940 HA

H 10.500 HA

W water

B bedrijfsterreinen

2001 AANTAL KRANEN

291

2001 TANKOPSLAG

33.000.0000M^3

2002 BINNENGEKOMEN [JANUARI – JUNI]

14.271

227.255.000 TON

2001 AANTAL SLEEPBOTEN

35

2001 AANTAL LOODSVAARTUIGEN

6

ACTIEVE BINNENVLOOT NEDERLAND

1996	1997	1998	1999	2000	2001
5.858.993	5.588.350	5.212.312	5.282.811	5.375.668	5.501.013

ROTTERDAM
STERKER DOOR STRIJD

dS+V, TNO, COS Rotterdam, CBS, Verkeerscirculatieplan 1982/1990 [Verkeersdienst Rotterdam], DCMR/Haven [website], Watertaxi [website], Verkeerspolitie Rotterdam, Eltis [European Local Transport Information Service] [website/rapportage 2001], -Scape, Adviesdienst Verkeer en vervoer, RET, Gemeentelijk Havenbedrijf Rotterdam [website].

Luuk Boelens (b. 1957) is an urban planner and since 2000 he has led the consultancy firm Urban Unlimited in partnership with Wies Sanders. He earned his Ph.D. with a thesis on Jürgen Habermas's theory of communicative practice and he is a writer and educator. His focus is on the network society and its consequences for mobility, governance, regional design and urban renewal.

Florian Boer (b. 1969) studied at the University of Technology, Eindhoven (TU/e). In 2000 he founded the design firm –scape, based in Rotterdam. The English suffix '–scape' shares the same origins as the modern Dutch 'scheppen', denoting the creation of space and a wide range of ideas. The firm's designs focus on human interaction, use and indication of movement. Their design style is intuitively expressive and narrative, but always based on careful observation. In addition to being a designer, Florian Boer also teaches at architecture academies and his writing has been published in various books and professional journals.

Frans Botma (b. 1973) worked for three years on environmental projects in Rotterdam, drawing on his training in urban planning. From this foundation, in recent years he has gone on to specialize in mobility-related environmental projects. His contributions to a broad spectrum of traffic projects, on scales ranging from local to European, are helping to build an environmentally conscious mobility programme.

Dolf Broekhuizen (b. 1965) is an architecture historian who writes about architecture and the preservation of historic buildings and monuments in the Netherlands. He was awarded his Ph.D. by the University of Groningen in 2000 for the thesis *De Stijl toen / J.J.P. Oud nu* ('De Stijl then / J.J.P. Oud now'), about architect J.J.P. Oud's involvement in the Reconstruction of the Netherlands after the Second World War. He is currently conducting research into open-air schools.

Martin Guit (b. 1970) trained as a traffic specialist and has worked on the infrastructure of Rotterdam for over eight years. He creates designs for large-scale infrastructure ranging from the port to the city centre. In recent years he has been reflecting on mobility in Rotterdam at a citywide structural level. In addition he is keenly interested in the city's history, which is what led to his contribution to this book.

Jannes Linders (b. 1955) is a documentary photographer who prefers not to specialize. His work demonstrates a broad interest for the built environment and the man-made landscape. He has produced series of urban landscapes in which no human being appears, but also series on such locations as Schiphol Airport, Brussels and Paris, in which great numbers of people are quite explicitly present.

Paul Meurs (b. 1963), managing director of Urban Fabric Schiedam, is an architect and researcher, gained his Ph.D. for *De moderne historische stad, ontwerpen voor vernieuwing en behoud, 1883–1940* ('The modern historic city, designing for renewal and preservation, 1883–1940'). Urban Fabric collaborates with Mecanoo Architects on research and concept development, including the design of new residential environments. Paul Meurs is also a participant in the Faculty of Architecture's working party on restoration at the Delft University of Technology (TU Delft).

Henk Oosterling (b. 1952) is a senior lecturer at the Faculty of Philosophy at the Erasmus University Rotterdam. He coordinates the research project 'Intermedialiteit. Over de grenzen van filosofie, kunst en politiek' ('Intermediality – Beyond the limits of philosophy, art and politics') for the university's Centre for Philosophy and Art (CFK). In addition to nineteenth-century and contemporary French philosophy, he lectures on the philosophy of art. His book *Radicale middelmatigheid* ('Radical mediocrity') recently went into a second printing.

Arnold Reijndorp (b. 1948) studied architecture at the TU Delft, worked for the Department for Urban Planning, Housing and Traffic in Rotterdam and taught urban sociology at the University of Amsterdam and the TU Berlin. He is a freelance researcher in cutting-edge urban planning and social and cultural developments in the network city. Recent publications (in association with other authors): *Buitenwijk. Stedelijkheid op afstand* ('Suburb – Remote Urbanity') (NAi Publishers, 1998) and *In search of new public domain* (NAi Publishers, 2001).

Pieter Schrijnen is an urban and traffic planner. His work initially involved mobility policy, strategic plans for traffic and transport and the coordination between spatial planning and traffic networks. In recent years he has been working on 'planning as learning', the innovative potential of people and organizations in traffic and transport and in spatial planning.

Harko Stolte (b. 1971) studied architecture at the TU Delft. After several years dedicated to the city of Rotterdam as an urban developer, he made a deliberate change to large-scale infrastructure projects. He is also active in shaping the traffic and transport policies of the city and region from a spatial-planning perspective.

Bas van Toledo (b. 1972) studied urban planning at the Polytechnic College of Utrecht (HTS Utrecht) and has worked as a traffic planner for the city of Rotterdam since 2001. During his travels across Asia and Africa he became fascinated with photographing everyday life. This, combined with his passion for the city of Rotterdam, led to this book's series of portraits of people in Rotterdam and their mobility choices.

Marc Verheijen (b. 1965) trained as a traffic specialist and as an architect. As an infrastructure designer he has participated in building the city of Rotterdam for 15 years. His preferred work area is at the interface of the various disciplines within spatial planning. This specific experience is what led to the initiative for this book.

ACKNOWLEDGEMENTS

This publication was made possible thanks to the support of the Department for Urban Planning, Housing and Traffic (dS+V) of the City of Rotterdam and was initiated by Marc Verheijen. The dS+V makes a significant contribution to the construction, housing and traffic policy of Rotterdam. As the design and planning entity responsible for these policy areas the dS+V has its sights set firmly on the future, considering the 'long-term perspective' as well as the issues of the day.

dS+V
Gemeente Rotterdam

Concept Paul Meurs and Marc Verheijen

Translation Andrew May **Copy Editing** Marianne Lahr **Graphic Design** Minke Themans
Printing and Lithography Die Keure **Production** Caroline Gautier **Publisher** Simon Franke

Picture credits Aeroview BV Rotterdam 142, 143; Stijn Brakkee 036 (portrait); Marco Okhuizen/HH 122; Familie Quack 034 (portrait); Joop Reyngoud 114. The other illustrations were supplied by the Department for Urban Planning, Housing and Traffic (dS+V), the City of Rotterdam and Rotterdam City Archives.

Thanks to Susan Bahadoersing, Wil Clerx, Jan van der Driessche, Evelien Elfring, Hans van Herwijnen, Inge van 't Hoogerhuijs, Leo de Jong, Rik Klink, Gerrit van der Kolk, Jan van der Kooij, Jan Kuipers, Chris Langen, Christel Leenen, Margot Lieftinck, Hans Lodder, Bertus Postma, Bart Roels, Fred de Ruiter, Bas Ruizeveld de Winter, Mariet Schoenmakers, Peter Volken Smidt en Jan van Teeffelen.

© NAi Publishers, Rotterdam, 2003 All rights reserved. No part of this publication may be reproduced, stored in a retrieval system, or transmitted in any form or by any means, electronic, mechanical, photocopying, recording or otherwise, without the prior written permission of the publisher. For works of visual artists affiliated with a CISAC-organization the copyrights have been settled with Beeldrecht in Amsterdam.
© 2003, c/o Beeldrecht Amsterdam

It was not possible to find all the copyright holders of the illustrations used. Interested parties are requested to contact NAi Publishers, Mauritsweg 23, 3012 JR Rotterdam, The Netherlands.

Available in North, South and Central America through D.A.P./Distributed Art Publishers Inc, 155 Sixth Avenue 2nd Floor, New York, NY 10013-1507, T +1 212 627 1999, F +1 212 627 9484, E dap@dapinc.com

Available in the United Kingdom and Ireland through Art Data, 12 Bell Industrial Estate, 50 Cunnington Street, London W4 5HB, T +44 208 747 1061, F +44 208 742 2319, E orders@artdata.co.uk

NAi Publishers is an internationally orientated publisher specialized in developing, producing and distributing books on architecture, visual arts and related disciplines. www.naipublishers.nl info@naipublishers.nl

Printed and bound in Belgium

ISBN 90 5662 301 X